The Courage
to Be Happy

The Courage
to Be Happy

by Dorothy Thompson

19   57

BOSTON

HOUGHTON MIFFLIN COMPANY

The Riverside Press Cambridge

To Bruce and Beatrice Gould

Foreword

NINETEEN FIFTY-SEVEN concludes twenty years during which I have contributed every month an essay to *The Ladies' Home Journal* — 240 in all, and the whole collection equal to six good-sized books! During the same period I was also writing three columns a week for fifty weeks of the year for a national press syndicate. This may seem a grueling life for any writer. It has been, and it continues to be, especially as I am not an "easy" writer. My thoughts (such as they are) only flow after a theme has been thoroughly developed in my mind, even to its verbal formulation. I have never sat frozen before a typewriter — or a ruled tablet, because I much prefer to write longhand, in pencil — but I go around with a glassy stare much of the time, which my family describes as "Mother doing her homework."

Actually, three columns a week are easier to write than one article a month. I had a long experience as a newspaper correspondent before I started writing a column, and the news always suggests a comment that will be published in a day or two, can be purely topical, and addressed to a general audience.

Writing for a monthly magazine is very different. What one writes will not appear for nearly eight weeks, and a theme suggested by current news will probably by then have been overtaken by new developments. *The Ladies' Home Journal*, with its vast circulation, may be read for weeks after an issue appears — abroad, in beauty parlors, doctors' offices, public libraries, and even at home. One must, therefore, try to write about more enduring things than a current budget debate or international crisis.

The Ladies' Home Journal also reaches a more limited *type* of audience than the national press. It is a "home" publication largely (though by no means exclusively) addressed to women. At first I thought it would be hard to write for women, because I had never before, as a writer, had any specific audience in mind, and had even been called a "man's" writer. But this apprehension proved groundless. I am a woman; month by month I have written about what interested *me*, and the mail has shown that (whether the correspondents agreed with me or not) they, too, have been interested in the same matters.

These essays have been more personal than anything else I have written, and the more personal, in general, the greater the response. Women — and men, too — have written me, "When I read you I feel as though we were talking with each other in the same room." To the extent that this is true I am pleased, the more so because letters from men and women all over this country and from places as far away as Australia and India have demonstrated that the conversation is not one-sided. Readers have offered me not only encouragement but many facts and stimulating ideas, for which I am deeply grateful.

In rereading what I have written over two decades, I have

been startled at the revelation of myself. I realize how deeply rooted I am in my own country, the home out of which I came, how all the experiences of my more adult years are checked and appraised against that background, how deeply skeptical I am of technological progress as the promise of human salvation and of many of the shibboleths that accompany it and promise by one means or another to bring about the millennium.

When I began writing these articles in the late 1930's, this conservative view was much less widespread than it is today. The world meanwhile has seen the failure of many mechanical formulas for human and mass salvation. But disillusion comes only to the illusioned. One cannot be disillusioned of what one never put faith in.

Life, it seems to me, now over sixty, is good, "be it stubbornly long or suddenly a mortal splendor" — and not only good, but wondrous and magical. And I am also convinced that it is purposeful; that "God," in Professor Einstein's words, "is not playing dice with the universe"; and that none of us need be the victim (or wholly the victim) of blind circumstances. There is a natural law and natural harmony that if we seek to discern we shall to some degree find. I have tried to testify to this.

This collection of only one-eighth of *The Ladies' Home Journal* essays was not made by me. It was made, first of all, by readers. I have chosen those articles which occasioned the greatest response as indicated by mail and requests to reprint. Apart from this, my secretary, Miss Virginia Shaw, helped me enormously by making an initial selection. My sister, Mrs. Howard Wilson, then read every word of the 240 articles and classified 76 of them as "Best" and "Second Best." Finally, I myself picked out thirty from their selections.

A writer who is still writing is seldom interested in what he or she said last week, last month, or ten (let alone twenty) years ago! So, this book appears only because so many readers have asked for it.

The arrangement is not in chronological order, but grouped by themes: essays on art or artists and literature; a group concerning children; a small one on age; the largest one on public affairs in a not topical sense; and, lastly, some observations on everyday life.

This book is dedicated, and properly, to Bruce and Beatrice Gould, the husband and wife who have edited *The Ladies' Home Journal* throughout my association with it. They have given me extraordinary liberty in the choice of subject matter. Where it has been necessary to cut articles, their paste-and-scissors personnel have often, to my mind, improved them; and when they have sent them back, as they have a few times for reconsideration, they have *always* been right.

A conscientious and perceptive editor is the writer's truest friend.

DOROTHY THOMPSON

Contents

Elderly Reflections

On Public Affairs

Observations of Everyday Life

On Art
and Artists

The Most Beautiful
Form of Courage

IN SUMMER we find more time to read — at least I do. There is less pressure, both of work and of those social obligations that pass for pleasure, and although my profession compels me to read copiously always, it is reading directed to a more or less immediate purpose. It is only in summer that I read books for their own sake.

Over the years I have from time to time encountered in British publications essays by Peter Quennell, who is a writer about writers. An exceptionally sympathetic and discerning one he is, and, being a lover of the art of writing, a good writer too — a fine writer, in fact — and one who has devoted himself to bringing to light again very good writers who, lacking whatever it is that makes and keeps men famous, are now forgotten or half-forgotten except by professional literati.

So I was pleased to find that Collins, London publisher, had collected and published over a score of Mr. Quennell's portraits and essays under the beguiling title, *The Singular Prefer-*

ence, which he took from one of Jane Austen's characters, Mr. Hurst in *Pride and Prejudice,* who expressed astonishment that a lady at a party declined a game of loo, saying she would stay below with a book. "Do you prefer reading to cards?" said he. "That is rather singular."

The first essay is on Joseph Joubert, whom I confess I had never heard of, or if I had, had forgotten, and I probably would have forgotten again this French writer who lived through the French Revolution and the Empire of Napoleon — and wrote continually but was so dissatisfied with his own work that he seldom finished what he began and was never published in his lifetime — were it not for something Mr. Quennell reported from a letter written by Joubert to his great (and unrequited) love, Pauline de Beaumont.

"One must learn to love life . . . " he insisted. "I am well content to tell you that I cannot admire you at leisure, and hold you in high esteem as I would wish, until I perceive in you the most beautiful of all forms of courage, the courage to be happy."

At this point I am content to leave Joubert and his Pauline — who did not become his, but fell in love with his friend and rival, the eminent Chateaubriand — to ponder what seems to me a remarkable phrase, "The courage to be happy." For never before had it occurred to me that it required courage to be happy, or that happiness is a demonstration of courage. Courage had always seemed to me to be that quality of mind that faces danger without fear, or endures pain, disappointment, grief, or loss with fortitude. I had thought of it, indeed, as the spirit that bravely endures *un*happiness.

But no. For M. Joubert, whom his biographers recognize as an exceedingly rare human spirit, the boy standing on the burning deck, valorous though he was, did not exhibit the most *beautiful* form of courage, nor all the unflinching burden-bearers whose virtues have been sung. Certainly no one could have accused the lady he thus reproved of lack of courage, if fortitude is its sign. An aristocrat by birth, but from the part of the French ruling class that had helped prepare the French Revolution, she had nevertheless lost home, friends, and family. Her father had been killed in the September massacres; her mother and brother had been guillotined, and when Joubert first encountered her she was sitting alone and disconsolate on the threshold of a peasant's cottage.

Her birth, upbringing, and natural quality prevented her from airing her misery and grievances, just as they were. She did not whine about her condition. She behaved nobly, that is to say, bravely, with fortitude and restraint.

But these are not synonyms for courage, though they are attributes of it. The lady — as we see from the other passage in her admirer's letters — had lost her faith in life. She had ceased to love life. And therefore however brave her mien she was *dis*couraged. Her friend sought to inspire, animate, inspirit her — in short to *en*courage.

Courage, it would seem, is nothing less than the power to overcome danger, misfortune, fear, injustice, while continuing to affirm inwardly that life with all its sorrows is good; that everything is meaningful even if in a sense beyond our understanding; and that there is always a tomorrow. It is part of the religious sense of life that sometimes exists in people without formal religion and is lacking in many religionists.

Joubert called the courage to be happy the most *beautiful* form of this supreme virtue. Certainly it beautifies its possessor, but it is also of all forms the most inspiriting to others. It does not ask for pity or even sympathy, but cheers.

Courage and compassion have been conjoined in discerning minds. Joseph Addison praised "unbounded courage and compassion join'd, temp'ring each other in the victor's mind," plainly indicating that the courage of the warrior-hero lacked something, in and of itself. But "courage," as the word's source indicates, is a virtue of the *heart*, not of the brain or nerves, and it has often been used as almost a synonym for spirit in its more superior manifestations. Rufus Choate, speaking of the battling colonials, mentioned "the courage of New England" that "was the courage of conscience," and never rose to "that insane passion the love of war for itself."

Spinoza thought that "temperance, sobriety, and presence of mind in danger" were each a species of courage — the first two representing resistance to temptation.

Charles Hamilton Aïdé, a late nineteenth-century writer, prayed "For calmness to remember, for courage to *forget*" — which comes close to the "courage to be happy." For obviously one cannot be happy while cherishing a grudge or nurturing a wrong. The "most beautiful form of courage" demands forgiveness — the "courage to forget."

And Robert Louis Stevenson, in a prayer many of us remember, asked for "courage, and gaiety, and the quiet mind," associating calmness and gaiety with courage though he did not make them synonyms.

But what — one thinks on — is happiness? Certainly it is not pleasure, though some people seem to think it is. I cannot help but think it is an inextinguishable sense of gratitude for and to life under even the most depressing circumstances. For there are no circumstances that can — or should — utterly blot out the recognition of goodness, the observation of beauty, and the memory of wonderful experiences. Happiness is a sort of continual act of faith, imposing a spontaneously accepted duty to be cheerful.

And thinking of M. Joubert's aphorism I remembered a great friend, an Austrian, who truly possessed the most beautiful form of courage. Fifteen years ago she lay dying in Switzerland. She had been known throughout Europe for her imaginative benevolences. After World War I she had been the first to conceive and carry out the idea of sending starving Austrian and German children to the neutral countries — Sweden, Norway, and Switzerland — where sympathetic families had given them both love and food. She had organized other relief measures on a grand scale, using her own money and raising it from others, and hundreds of thousands of Austrians and Germans had been her beneficiaries.

When Hitler marched into Austria she was in Copenhagen, where she had just undergone an operation for cancer of the breast. She was informed that her homes had been confiscated, and that she could not return, because she was a Jewess. Later some of the children she had sent to Norway returned the hospitality of their hosts by coming back with the Nazi armies — especially picked because they knew Norwegian. All Europe was at war.

She had risen from her sickbed with an open wound and gone to Paris to aid the refugees streaming from Austria. Her husband had died of a stroke induced by shock. And now she, too, lay dying. For the breast disease had healed, to reappear as cancer of the bone.

I went to sit at her bedside, expecting to find an embittered woman who for half a generation of service had received the basest ingratitude. The friends who were with her, voluntarily sharing her exile, told me that her physician had explained her excruciating pain to her as arthritis. But alone with her, I quickly discovered that she was playing the rather gruesome game for their sakes. Only to me she said, "I am dying, you know. I shall never see you again after you leave, but how wonderful that you came to me!"

I had know her as a woman of brains, warmth, and fantastic energy. But the woman at whose side I sat in the brief hours when she was awake from narcotics was a saint. Never had I seen her face so radiantly beautiful.

I had gone to comfort her as best I could, but I was full of bitterness, for I had loved Germany and hated now her hideous face. But my friend scolded, cheered, and comforted me.

There was not one spark of resentment in her. "Germany has gone crazy," she said. "Such things have happened before — an epidemic of madness. But it will pass. Germany will be terribly defeated. But you must not hate. Everyone will hate, but there must be some who do not hate though they fight like tigers. Hate will corrode reconciliation. But there must be reconciliation, sometime. People change. I assure you they do. Fight Nazism — but never abandon hope and belief in the Germans!"

And I saw that nothing that had happened, to her or to her friends or her country, had shaken her faith in all the peoples of humanity.

But I have taken here an extreme case of the courage to be happy, and I am not sure that it is a good illustration. Perhaps it is easier to mobilize such sublimity in the face of death than to manifest a more prosaic form of it through care-burdened life. Most of us, I think, respond more nobly to great crises than to small harassments.

Yet who of us does not see all around us, people exercising the "most beautiful form of courage"? One observes it as often — I think more often — among simple people of limited means and education than among the more fortunate, complicated, and refined. One wonders how some of these people endure their cares and disappointments: the layoff from work, economic insecurity, a crippled or mentally deficient child, the frustration of ambition, the foreclosure of painfully accumulated property.

But one finds in families whose members love each other a capacity that goes beyond endurance, that responds to every little windfall of good luck with seemingly exaggerated joy, and that never for a moment stops hoping and believing; a spirit that can be happy merely because the sun shines, or because a neighbor speaks a warm affectionate word, or a child laughs.

These people do not appear to us as heroes, and the dour sometimes chide them, in their minds, as too "happy-go-lucky." But they are the savor of human society — and unconsciously we know it. What else do we mean when we say of a person, "He (or she) is the salt of the earth"?

Do we not thus recognize a person with the beautiful courage to be happy?

Thank you, M. Joubert — and Mr. Quennell.

The Miracle of an Artist

DURING THE past fall and winter, tens of thousands of New Yorkers and visitors from outside passed through the Metropolitan Museum of Art to see an extraordinary exhibition of drawings and paintings by a man who died in France over sixty years ago. On the walls of the Metropolitan Museum hung the story of a life and the expression of a human passion, the impact of it so terrific that after two hours of gazing, one's heart palpitated and one's knees trembled. The paintings are the record of a man beginning somberly, in darkness, and moving steadily into light, until, gazing straight into the sun, he tore the veil from nature to present an incandescent world of almost unbearable glory and beauty, in which all form is movement and all things are energy, a world where nature palpitates and sings.

The paintings of Vincent Van Gogh are a miracle. No one before him saw the world as he saw it, and no one having seen it through his eyes can ever see it in the same way again. He was, perhaps, all unconsciously, the first painter of the atomic age. He knew nothing of physics or of mathematics. His knowledge of the world came not through the brain but through the eye. Yet he certainly saw a world in which a chair, a flower, a plowed field, a tree, were not stable matter but vibrant neutrons of energy and light. If one looks at his greatest paintings close to the canvas they are a formless chaos. When one moves back the forms leap forward, forms of a nature caught in movement, no moment being like the preceding one or the one to follow. No one before Van Gogh caught in painting, I think, the fourth dimension of time.

What he saw destroyed him. Standing in a plowed field at the age of thirty-seven, ill, and mad, he put a bullet through his heart. No doubt he saw more than ever he could paint, and more than it is permitted man to see. Only a fragment of his vision is transmitted to us. But it is a vision beginning in sorrow and rising into joy — joy beyond happiness, joy exciting, disturbing, awesome, beautiful, and with an undertow of terror.

Vincent Van Gogh wanted to see God. Deeply religious, parsonage-born, in a Dutch Protestant family who had connections to the art world through members who were dealers, and who for generations had never been without a pastor member, he first sought God through the Bible and through theological training, in preparation for the ministry, and in work among the poorest and lowliest Flemish miners and weavers. Of this period, before he had realized himself as a painter, he leaves a pictorial *de profundis* of patient, long suffering human misery. He paints with pity to dissolve his colors and they are the colors of the static earth.

But Vincent Van Gogh did not find God in Church, with its respectabilities and, to his consciousness, hypocrisies and coldness of heart; nor even in humanity as such, though he found Him in the human mystery. God, he found, was life. He was in all living things, and above all in nature. And Van Gogh's eye saw, for all the pain and suffering of humanity, the glory of life and the truth of the glory. And that is what he has transmitted to us.

His own life was a record of personal frustration, material wretchedness, and universal misunderstanding. From the time he left his father's house to the day he ended his life, he never earned even pocket money. His entire family, with one exception — his brother Theo — regarded him as a black sheep and useless dreamer. And even Theo, as we see from Vincent's letters, often wavered in his faith. The artist did not accept their judgment debonairly, and for most of his life their judgment of him was his own. His teachers — when he was able to get them through Theo — scolded him that what he did was neither "charming" nor "salable." He never had money enough to marry, though he longed for a home. His cousin, whom he loved flamingly, turned him down, and for the love of women — and for his models — he had only poor outcast creatures, coarse and to any other eye ugly, yet their portraits hang in the greatest art collections today. He was often ill, perpetually humiliated, frightfully lonely, and in the last years of his life quite incurably mad. Although he lived in the vast museum of art treasures which Europe was and is, he never saw Greece or Rome, or the glorious paintings of the Renaissance in Florence and Venice.

The great burst of his genius — and his whole life as a
painter was compressed into ten years — came when he removed to the sleepy town of Arles, in the French Provence
country of color and sun, and there he painted his greatest
pictures, living after a time in a hospital, painting what he saw
through his window, until finally he was transferred to the
insane asylum at St. Rémy, twenty miles away, occasionally
let out to paint the surrounding orchards and fields, living
the rest of his life in recovery and relapse, and painting when
well, in a sort of trance. All that he painted in this period is
alive and growing. His trees are not standing but growing or
fading like his wheat fields and his people. He needed to
search nowhere for things to paint — he painted what was all
around him.

His view of the world has been called romantic. But his
letters reveal great refinement of intellect and no painter ever
put himself through more austere disciplines, attaching enormous importance to drawing, if it only were drawing from
living models. Poverty, indifference to convention, and lack
of capacity to cope with everyday life made his personal life
disorderly, but he was not disorderly in his work, though he
pursued it with febrile intensity, in a conscious race against
time.

He hated his dependency on his brother, who was not very
well off himself. There was never enough money for both
the most primitive comforts and the materials of his art, and
he starved himself to buy paint and canvas. From critics, art
dealers, and the public he received no encouragement. When
he died he had sold only one painting. His total earnings from
ten years of the most intense and inhuman effort were about
one hundred dollars. But the exhibition assembled in New
York by the Metropolitan Museum of Art and the Art Institute of Chicago from museums and private collectors all

over the Western world, is valued at $3,000,000, and by no means contains all his great works.

But I am not writing a posthumous success story, but trying rather to inquire into what constitutes a great life. Vincent Van Gogh not only left the record of himself in his paintings, but he left a complete autobiography in his extraordinary letters to Theo, published last year for the first time in America, and edited by Irving Stone. These letters express almost inutterable anguish. But they also express almost inutterable aspiration and ecstatic joy. Minutely he describes to his brother the color, shape, and sounds of things. A walk, in an undistinguished landscape, fills him with rhapsody. And incredible patience possesses him, and he is always humble. Although he cries, "I want more soul, more love, more heart!" (in life and in his work), he feels that in spite of all his misery, life has granted him the *privilege* to be an artist. He commiserates with his brother that he does not paint and therefore misses so much! He tries to communicate to him, not only his material anguish but his spiritual joy. Not for an instant does he rail against God. He affirms His existence; he sees nobility in the poorest and most fallen creatures, who "cannot," he declares, "be destined for the worms."

What is happiness? In our own age we think of it as comfort and the sum of material things, and our President, in a State of the Union message, encouraged us to believe in a trillion-dollar production of those things by the year 2000!

Happiness is difficult without some comfort. Van Gogh would not, I believe, have been a less great artist had he had enough to eat. But happiness is *not* joy. Joy springs *only* from creative activity, and by some mystery we do not understand creation is almost always integrated with pain. All intense effort — the effort of the mother in childbirth, of the athlete, of the scholar, working in intense intellectual concentration, or of the saint in his intense spiritual concentration, of the artist, of the craftsman — has in it an element of pain, for effort stems from the urge to rise above one's own limitations, to do what is beyond one's strength and capacities. Effort is by nature *uncomfortable*. Yet only through effort does anyone find exhilaration and joy.

There is even an effort of the senses — of seeing, tasting, smelling, hearing — without which the senses become numbed. In the rush after material comforts, through which we expend not effort but time, we throw away the gifts with which nature endowed us all. The English poet W. H. Davies properly commented:

> "*A poor life this if, full of care,*
> *We have no time to stand and stare.*"

Through my husband, who is an artist, I received a new pair of eyes. Eyes, for instance, which saw *for the first time* the New York sky — except on overcast days a curiously luminous, ever-changing, *southern* sky. And it comes free — no entrance charge.

Some effort is necessary for the appreciation even of everyday things. I watch office girls swallowing a drugstore lunch, and it is clear they do not taste what they are eating. Yet, if one *thinks* about it, it is the simplest things that taste best: the chewy crust of good bread, the crunchy tartness of an apple. How much of joy one loses who reduces food to nourishment alone.

Our world is full of "entertainment" — the movies, the radio, now television. But through much bad or banal music, our ears become numb to all music; through a surfeit of inferior melodrama, we become blind to the drama of life. In art, as with Gresham's currency law "Bad money drives out good," bad art debases the *currency* of art. The music goes past our ears, but leaves them deafer; the movie goes past our eyes, but leaves them blinder. Almost all entertainment is an anodyne. But art, even to the concentrated observer, is an *experience* — exhilarating, but rarely comfortable.

And, worst of all perhaps, our generation has no time for contemplation; meditation is a lost art, and this may account for the extraordinary policies of modern statesmen. And without previously cultivated contemplation, solitude is terrifying. Nothing becomes more frightening than to be alone with oneself, a stranger with whom one has never become intimate. Then old age approaches, an awful specter of loneliness to those who have never found joy in being alone.

To men and women of genius, Van Gogh among them, who died before I was born, I owe vicarious joy, and an intensification of experience, and therefore of life. Because they lived, and suffered, and worked, all men after them can, if they will, live more than they would otherwise have done. And that, too, is part of the miracle.

The Woman Poet*

ON OCTOBER 7 we drove toward Austerlitz, New York, on Route 22, going back to New York from our home in Vermont. My husband was driving, and I said, "Maxim, let's stop and see Edna Millay."

* This essay was greatly cut for space in *The Ladies' Home Journal.* Here it appears as originally written.

"No," said Maxim, not slowing down at all. "She does not want to see us. She does not want to see anyone. She has closed the door in the face of her most intimate friends. You wrote her twice and she didn't answer. She doesn't want to see you."

"Why should she write?" I asked. "The letters didn't require an answer. Besides, writers don't like to write letters. It's not idle curiosity — you know that. She means so much to me — not as an intimate friend — as an artist — a very great artist. There is just no one with her. One could, at least — if she were willing — take her some food and drink, and cook it, and wash up the dishes and sweep the floor. That sort of thing. I can think of no one for whom I would rather do some sort of — well — menial service."

"If the house is untidy, she won't want you to see it," said Maxim firmly. "And besides, you know her hours, how she turns night into day and vice versa."

"Yes," I said, and smiled to myself. "She weeds her lazy lettuce by the light of the moon."

"She does what?" asked Maxim.

> "*Before she has her floor swept*
> *Or her dishes done,*
> *Any day you'll find her*
> *A-sunning in the sun.*
>
> "*It's long after midnight*
> *Her key's in the lock,*
> *And you'll never see her chimney smoke*
> *Till past ten o'clock!*
>
> "*She digs in her garden*
> *With a shovel and a spoon,*
> *She weeds her lazy lettuce*
> *By the light of the moon.*

"It's by Edna. Called "Portrait by a Neighbour" — and, of course, a portrait of herself, as a neighbor might regard her. You are probably right. She will have been up all night, and now she is asleep. She was always like that — no, not always. Sometimes she would get up at dawn because she adored the earliest morning, when everything smells so wonderful and nobody at all around. She just doesn't like *normal* hours."

"She has locked herself in," Maxim said, "to write as long as she can go on doing so, and then — to die. She is going to die. She is going to die because she cannot live without Eugene, and, even more importantly, she cannot live without writing poetry. All artists are like that. They can survive almost anything — poverty, heartbreak, unrequited love — they turn that all into poetry, or pictures, or what not. But when they fear their gifts have left them, then they die."

"But she still writes lovely poetry."

"By whose standards?" asked Maxim, who is an artist. "She has written reams she never published. She is a craftsman and no one can deceive her about her work — not to surpass herself is failure. She thinks she cannot surpass herself."

> *"Who can tell if Shelley's gold*
> *Had survived it to grow old?"*

I quoted softly.

"Do you know all her work by heart?" Maxim asked, astonished.

"No, of course not," I said. "But a great deal of it. I don't know why — I never tried to memorize anything. But she had ways of saying things you never could forget — at least I never could — nor many others, especially women. And now I am *terribly* worried about her. I don't know why. But I am worried. I have some sort of premonition."

"If you insist," said Maxim. "But I have a premonition too, and it tells me to let Edna alone."

Maxim's premonitions are better than mine, and so I did not insist he stop at the narrow dirt road that winds rockily up to "Steepletop," where Edna St. Vincent Millay lived. It was true that I was never one of Edna's intimate friends. Of late years I had seen her hardly at all. We had been together at Steepletop some five years ago, when Maxim painted her portrait — not at all a conventional portrait, but a most arresting one. "You have a Gothic face," Maxim had said, squinting critically. "Like a potato. Bumpy, I mean, over the eyebrows, and on the cheekbones, definitely potato."

Certainly no one had ever before compared Miss Millay, who had a brow like Beethoven's, "more hair than she needs, in the sun it's a woe to me . . . and a mouth like a valentine," to a potato, but she was enchanted. "I really have," she said, "and a Gothic belly too — a little waist and then a definite round mound." And she looked at herself in the glass, as though she had never seen herself before. She looked at herself often, in the glass, I remembered, as though trying to fathom somthing that was to herself unfathomable, and once I saw her, when she was making up her mouth, throw the lipstick right into the glass with a cry of anger and pain, and splinter it.

On the way, beyond Austerlitz, I recalled these things. She had liked the portrait very much. Afterward it had been sold to the Syracuse Museum and I had written to tell her that. That was one of the letters she had not answered. We talked of the weekend when the portrait was painted. She was very ill then, very near one of those breakdowns into which she periodically sank, and from which she periodically emerged, apparently unscathed, with the extraordinary vitality which was inbred.

After just such breakdowns during which there was much wringing of hands among her friends, she would rise like the dragonfly from the weedy shallows, and one could see her pushing a wheelbarrow up a steep hill, running, in shorts, like a barefoot boy, her red hair that never grayed streaming in the wind, looking timeless and ageless, although she had seen fifty years.

In moods of discouragement — for whatever reasons — she abused herself abominably. It was the despair of her friends, and must have been of her husband. If so he never showed it before others, and I think rarely to her.

Eugene Jan Boissevain was a remarkable man, and their marriage a remarkable relationship. It is not sufficient to record that for the best twenty-five years of his life he devoted himself entirely to his poet wife, waiting on her hand and foot, acting as husband, nurse, cook, business manager, and above all friend, to a whimsical genius sometimes as petulant and imperious as the child Cleopatra whom Caesar first met in Egypt; sometimes a witch, with a trace of the sinister, stormy, turbulent, and as unreckonable as the sea — her native element; sometimes a lost and tragic soul.

Meek, patient women have given up their personal lives time out of number for men of genius, and the biographies of the great pay them proper, if slightly bored praise. The opposite is rare. So to state in prosaic terms the role of the poet's husband suggests an analogy: a meek and servile man, slightly epicene, meekness and servility being no manly virtues, serving a famous woman, who, as the ugly phrase has it "wore the pants."

Nothing could be further from the truth of this relationship, which was out of another era and time. Eugene Boissevain was handsome, virile, cultivated, proud, and self-contained. In the old remodeled farmhouse, with its sweeping mountain view and its lovely tangled garden, full of the flashes of birds' wings, and the slumberous music of bees, where

grew all the herbs and flowers the poet loved — tansy and
mignonette, verbena and creeping phlox, lavender and tall
spires of delphinium in all the blues of painted windows, these,
and the loved and tolerated weeds, the black-eyed Susan, the
misty Queen Anne's lace — no servant set foot to conform
a household to the tyranny of the clock.

Yet there was nothing "Bohemian" about this place, but
comely order. Eugene was a superb and most refined cook,
who cooked as men do, who love the art, with much less fuss
than women, who so often require dour concentration. The
kitchen was also a salon, full of wit and laughter, and dinner
was served on beautiful porcelain, in candlelight, with a
bottle of exquisite wine.

How to describe one's impression of such a relationship?
It was as though a throneless queen, presiding at a court of
beauty and love, peopled half with phantoms of the fantasy,
had picked from among her many courtiers a favorite, and
appointed him Master of the Queen's Household, Lord-in-
Waiting, Chief Equerry, Chancellor of the Exchequer, and
Court Jester — and thus ennobled him.

Queens — even queens of the spirit — must not be bothered by the drab details of life. In later years the poet's
knight was also something of a wizard. There were long
years in which the singing voice was still, and the great vogue
the poet had enjoyed in the twenties and thirties died down.
Edna, like a queen, never touched money, never wrote a
check, never paid a bill, nor had any notion of what her
income was, nor that what the Lord of the Household had
brought to her was long since spent. Yet, though the jour-
neys abroad — and to the opera, the symphony, the gay and
splendid restaurants — were curtailed or halted, she slept
between fresh linen and fed "upon strawberries, sugar and
cream" with the music of Beethoven in the clear rooms,
and the laughter of her favorite cheering her gloomy moods.

This sounds preposterous in the twentieth century, but that is the way it was, and this hard and cruel century was not the only time of either of them.

What *was* her time?

It is the peculiar gift of the poet to telescope many times into one. Wherever beauty walked is in their time. The fair youth on the Grecian urn never faded for Keats, "For ever wilt thou love, and she be fair!" The rose that grew in Omar's garden, or in Homer's, grew in Miss Millay's, who wrote that her own love would have lost some part "had Helen died, or stayed at home in Greece."

The little girl who flat on her stomach in a bare Maine cottage had turned the pages of dusty books drawn from a small town library, telling of "rose-red cities half as old as time," was transported out of that town and out of that age. The village girl striding a windswept island off the Maine coast walked hand in hand with another island girl, whose eyes had looked out upon the Ionian Sea, long centuries ago, and whose name was Sappho. The woman who broke her heart in tempestuous, unwise love, broke it with a woman who dying long years ago upon a Cornish coast, was named Isolde. The ladies of the courts of love and beauty of the miraculous thirteenth century held converse with the pig-tailed child, who did not live in the past but brought the past into the present. And a biographer may one day celebrate that unique but little noted institution of American life — the big and little public libraries that hand out their magic of thought and rhyme to every snub-nosed urchin with some spark of divine hunger, from Maine to California.

So if this household and this relationship seems strange, it is strange only to those who live between the brief dawn and twilight of one limited time, not with the riches, the conventions, and the rebellions of two thousand years, selecting with delicate discrimination what is proper to their natures.

"Are they not isolated and lonely?" people asked wonderingly. A foolish question. The imaginative only child who invents his playmates is half a poet. The protean mind is always peopled. Eugene Boissevain lived with a poet, and therefore lived with an imagination.

There must have been enormous compensations for the burdens, sometimes of grief and always of care, that he carried, since his spirit remained blithe as a skylark's. There certainly were. Miss Millay was an extraordinary creature. She not only possessed the greatest natural lyric talent given to any American in this generation — her first published poem, "Renascence," written by an adolescent was pure inspiration, poured out in one gush, with hardly a word to change — but she had a most penetrating intelligence, and the gift of evoking the most passionate and tender love. When she was happy, charmed, or enchanted, she had an indescribable radiance. She lit up, incandescent as a Christmas tree. She was a most exciting conversationalist, whose mind could roam through music, philosophy, art, and even politics. On the latter she was somber, with a prophetic premonition of coming times of trouble. Long before there was talk of atom bombs she wrote of a reeling planet absolutely destroyed, in "The Blue-Flag in the Bog." And long before World War II, in one of the finest of her cycles of Sonnets, she wrote "Epitaph for the Race of Man," knowing that none of the catastrophes of nature — not flood, nor fire, nor earthquake, nor the erupting volcano — would lay low man's dauntless stubborn brow, but only his own hand against his brothers and himself.

And when she gave pain, as she often did, only the mean-hearted could be unforgiving. For pain and compassion were the essence of her nature — pain and compassion, and beauty and love. She had a lovely speaking voice — "like a string of colored beads, or steps leading into the sea." She was not beautiful. Her mouth was too large, her chin too short, her forehead too high. Her eyes were not large, but strange: more green than blue, sometimes dark, even murky, sometimes light and clear as aquamarines. Her figure was slight and somewhat childish. She had beautiful hands and feet. Once when we were together in Budapest and she had got a check from Frank Croninshield, for one of the hack pieces she was writing for *Vanity Fair* under the pen name of Nancy Boyd, she left her hotel bill unpaid to buy herself thirteen pairs of shoes. She lined them up and gazed with ecstasy. (As I recall it, I paid the hotel bill, and — more significant — without the slightest resentment.)

She was not beautiful; she was a great deal more than that. She could create the illusion of beauty. She did not create it as an actress creates it. If she *felt* beautiful, she became beautiful. She was always beautiful when she was in love. And she was in love a great many times.

I suppose no woman has written more daringly of love than Edna St. Vincent Millay. It was, of course, one source of her enormous vogue. She broke into song in the twenties at a time when a whole flock of novelists and poets were defying the American puritan tradition, challenging the Philistines and astonishing the bourgeoisie. The author of "What lips my lips have kissed" was the talk of the town and the occasion of the most delicious gossip. Yet if that had been all there was to it, her first editions would not before her death have become collector's items. She wrote of love honestly, beautifully, cleanly, with both a passion and a delicacy unsurpassed. She spoke for every woman who has ever broken her heart — and what woman has not? Furthermore, she really loved, and the price she paid was not gossip and scandal; she was famous enough to live that down — and, indeed, it enhanced her sales. The price she paid was anguish. The only reward she had, and we have, too, was that out of often unrequited love, like Heine, she has written "these songs."

Some of her sonnets of brokenhearted love are of the utmost resignation and simplicity. Such are the exquisite "Pity me not" and "Time does not bring relief," each of which speaks an experience every woman knows.

And this must be said: Miss Millay wrote as a woman. It would have been as futile as for Sappho or Emily Dickinson or Elinor Wylie to have sought to hide her sex under some man's name — as "George" Eliot or "George" Sand. She saw things with a womanly mind and womanly intuition. All the handwriting is feminine. Even the things she noticed were things that men pass by — the homely jelly glass, the kettle, the broom, and the ways of men that men themselves never see. And she wrote of *woman's* love.

The young poet who scandalized the drawing rooms never penned a word that by any stretch of the imagination could be called pornographic or licentious, and rarely was she flippant. Her flippant quips, popular around the campuses in the twenties and thirties, are her worst — and least representative — expression. But the great testimonies of love, best expressed in the sonnets, and above all in the fifty-two that compose the volume *Fatal Interview* are surpassed by no woman and few men who ever wrote of love. In some of these there is, indeed, "Love like a burning city in the breast," immensely ennobled by its unregenerate wholeness, the love of queens who have thrown away a kingdom for an embrace, and never repented.

In the summer of 1949 Eugene Boissevain suddenly died, and it was that which was implicit in the conversation with my husband as we drove through Austerlitz. The poet went back to the empty house, remote in the mountains, with no servant, no telephone, even, nothing but a caretaker who did not live in the house, and no more a Lord of the Household. Two weeks after our hesitation in Austerlitz, she was found dead. No soul had entered the house during the eight hours in which her body lay at the foot of the stairs, struck down by a heart attack immediately fatal. Apparently she had died on her way to bed, at 3.30 in the morning. She loved life and hated death. She had written that she would liefer be a cripple in a wheel chair than die; she would struggle with death; she would "take it hard." But death was swifter — and more merciful — than she imagined this enemy. So many had loved her, and she had loved so many. But death, invading, found her absolutely alone. And absolutely alone, except for her peopled mind, she had always been, in the most profound sense — which was perhaps the source of her anguish even in love. For there was always that other love, that strongest and most compelling passion: Poetry, the singing line.

> *Wine from these grapes I shall be treading surely*
> *Morning and noon and night until I die.*
> *Stained with these grapes I shall lie down to die.*

She trod the wine of pure art out of the grapes of her own heart's blood and her wrung mind. And so it was when she died.

But, it seems to me, she wrote her finest work when she moved from the lyric born of the personal experience of joy and anguish to the impersonal expression of the joy and anguish of the world, and brought a penetrating mature intelligence to the direct expression of the heart and of the senses. None of her love sonnets is finer than "Country of hunchbacks!" which expresses scathing scorn of mediocrity, or "To Jesus on His Birthday," or "Euclid alone has looked on Beauty bare." Long before T. S. Eliot wrote *The Cocktail Party*, she produced *Conversation at Midnight*, in which all the crossing and conflicting currents of modern thought —

liberalism, capitalism, communism, Christianity — are expressed in the most difficult medium for such expression, poetry. And expressed with startling objectivity. Who among the conversationalists represents the poet? Perhaps Ricardo, because he is the gentlest and least cruel. For hatred of cruelty is another consuming passion to be found through all her work, and not only in "The Murder of Lidice," written for the Writer's War Board during the war, which, like most writing inspired from outside and for political purposes, never quite came off.

> *Cruel of heart [she wrote] lay down my song . . .*
> *Not for you was the pen bitten,*
> *And the mind wrung, and the song written.*

She was conscious, too, of the anguish of the world in this most cruel century. "The anguish of the world is on my tongue." The consciousness was present from the beginning — in the very first poem through which she attracted fame: "Renascence." She was just nineteen when she wrote that, living on the Maine coast, in dire poverty, with a mother who went out doing practical nursing to support three daughters deserted by a gambler father, and she herself working as a typist when she could. She told me that once guests and "help" in a summer inn where her sister Norma worked had a common party, and everyone was invited to perform a stunt, and she sat down at the piano and played a tune and sang a little song. Upon inquiry she confessed she had written the words and music herself and, when pressed, confessed she had written other things. Yes, she was willing to recite one. And sitting on the piano stool (in a childish dress), with her auburn hair streaming down her back, she began,

"All I could see from where I stood
Were three long mountains and a wood . . . "

the opening lines of "Renascence."

One of the guests at this extraordinary occasion was Miss Caroline B. Dow, who promptly decided to take the young genius out of her limited and impoverished surroundings and give her a college education. The poem she had recited was later acclaimed by the critic Louis Untermeyer as the greatest poem written in America since Whitman's "When Lilacs Last in the Dooryard Bloom'd." I do not agree with Mr. Untermeyer, nor think it anything like the finest of Miss Millay's poems. But there is in it, as there is in so many of her poems, a cosmic sense of human suffering, and incomparable singing lines.

Yet when I recall what I remember by heart, they are mostly lines recording simple and homely things. The gray eyes of the mother — how the sacrificing mother haunts her, unforgotten always, perhaps dearer to the poet than any other human being ever was. The mother of "The ballad of the Harp-Weaver." The observation of nature — the "moss invading the stone," "the flight of the golden flicker with his wing to the light," the "drum of a beak on the rotted willow," the "hinge of the lid on a spider's eye" (Is it little? It is greater than death), the bobolink, "a little bird gone daft," the "catbirds that call through the long afternoon," the "eager vines" that "go up the rocks and wait," the "round-faced roses, pink and petulant," and she herself, "sacked by the wind and rain." How much of rain there is in her poems — "I would I were alive again, to kiss the fingers of the rain" — how much of birds, and flowers and herbs, and rocks and wild pastures and, above all, the sea. She writes with nostalgia:

No matter what I say,
All that I really love
Is the rain that flattens on the bay,
And the eel-grass in the cove . . .

There is something else to note. The generation of the twenties in which she emerged was decrying the United States. America was regarded as Greater Zenith, filled with Babbitts, and the spiritual home of the American intellectual and artistic elite was on the Left Bank of the Seine. (But Babbitt finally went crazy . . . not in America but in Germany.) Miss Millay also went to Paris; it was there I met her, and in Vienna and Budapest that I came to know her best. She was made much of in Europe — not only in the Left Bank cafés, but in the embassies and in the refined society that welcomes talent and genius. But she who carried with her the inheritance of the culture of the race, was still as American and New England as ragged robin and steamed clams. She spoke the English of Elizabethans; she spoke beautiful French, and translated the poems of Baudelaire. She spoke fair German and knew the literature of most European countries. But she hardly wrote a lyric that derived its central inspiration from anything but American sights, sounds, smells, tastes, and ideas. She liked American men, though she married a man born in the Netherlands who was American by firm preference. She liked homely, even trivial things, about America — such as that "Americans don't put a dead man at the top of the bed under the pillow," a comment on the hated European bolster. She traveled widely, and was always homesick, and never for brilliant cities, but for the mountains or the sea — not the Alps but the Berkshires; not the tideless Mediterranean but the rocky coast of Maine. However tall and wide the tree of her spirit might grow and

spread, its roots dug deep into American soil. She knew
every bird that flies and every flower and weed that grows in
her native New England. Let her but sit still on a sea-washed
rock, on the wild island off the Maine coast, which was a second home, and gulls would fly around her head. She wrote
in a poem that she hoped she would die at sea and her body
be given to the sea; or she imagined herself in death as ash
drifting on the wind:

> *And you will say, seeing me,*
> *What a strange thing,*
> *Like a plum petal*
> *Or a butterfly's wing.*

Her elements were surely fire and water: she was self-con-
suming, and self-drowned.

One ponders on the inscrutability of the fairy godmother,
who puts the star of genius on so few brows — on the child
in a palace cradle; a child bred of a family otherwise as stodgy
as pot roast; the plowboy among yokels; the son of some
petty clerk, presumably destined like his father to hunch
over files and bills of lading; or the girl of Irish-American
parentage born in a dingy flat in a sleepy seaswept town in
Maine. Nature, in her most prodigal gifts, is without snobbery, even the inverted snobbery that scorns the wellborn,
which is one reason, perhaps, that great poets are seldom
class-conscious.

And what does she endow the poet with? In Miss Millay's
case, with the hypersensitive senses of the animals — the
ear of the deer, the smell of the hound — and with the sensibility that is refined from the sensual; with the swift mind
that darts, not plods, to the heart of truth; with such antennae
as we cannot yet explain to receive messages that others hear

not, from the past, the future, and from living time; and with hearts that breaking spill their blood in roses.

And what shall one write in elegy of her to whom this humdrum writer — for so I feel myself to be — owes so much of beauty and of insight?

No epitaph.

> *I am not willing you should go*
> *Into the earth where Helen went.*

But rather a response to the urgent cry she uttered in "The Poet and His Book" — *Do not let me die!*

> *Stranger, pause and look;*
>   *From the dust of ages*
> *Lift this little book,*
>   *Turn the tattered pages,*
> *Read me, do not let me die!*
>   *Search the fading letters, finding*
>   *Steadfast in the broken binding*
> *All that once was I!*
>
> .   .   .   .
>
> *Women at your toil,*
>   *Women at your leisure*
> *Till the kettle boil,*
>   *Snatch of me your pleasure,*
> *Where the broom-straw marks the leaf;*
>   *Women quiet with your weeping*
>   *Lest you wake a workman sleeping,*
> *Mix me with your grief!*
>
> .   .   .   .
>
> *Suns that shine by night,*
>   *Mountains made from valleys, —*
> *Bear me to the light,*

Flat upon your bellies
By the webby window lie,
Where the little flies are crawling,
Read me, margin me with scrawling,
Do not let me die!

Dear poet, as long as hearts love and mouths laugh, and flowers blossom, and the rain washes the pane, and the young spring breaks, and hearts being hungry search for solace, and minds for insight, and the ear for song — these will not let you die!

Nor so long as I live will I.

The Old Bible and the New

I REMEMBER VIVIDLY a moment in my childhood as an event of more than passing importance.

Every morning before breakfast we assembled in the sitting room and my father read a passage from the Bible, followed by a prayer. These family prayers did not appeal to me as a child hungry for her breakfast, an absent-minded child, too, whose thoughts were usually woolgathering. But on this particular morning my father started to read the Book of Job. The dramatic story caught my attention, and when he would have closed the book, I begged him to go on, so his voice conveyed — doubtless with many skippings — the tale

of Job's temptations, trust, and woes. But somewhere, as
my father read, I became excitedly aware of something more
than the story: of the beauty, and glory of words; of the
images they can evoke and the thoughts they can enkindle.
In short, on that morning, I discovered for the first time inspired literature.

Why I should first have found it in the Book of Job I do
not know, for I had been exposed practically from infancy
to great passages of the Bible and of the English classics read
aloud. I suppose my mind had become ripe to begin to receive what it had hitherto rejected or ignored. Certainly
I did not understand a tenth of what I was hearing, but I
understood enough to make me want to know more, and the
magnificent cadences, the pictures of all manner of living
things, Job's majestic descriptions of God — a God so close
and real that he argued with him — were not lost on my
childish ears and limited understanding.

Since that time I have been a constant reader of the Bible,
and especially of some parts of it — Ezekiel and Job, Isaiah
and the Unknown Prophet, Amos, Micah, Jeremiah, Ecclesiastes, the Psalms, and all of the New Testament, and from
much reading and rereading many passages and a few whole
chapters I know by heart.

It was therefore with immense interest and anticipation
that I picked up the new "Revised Standard Version" issued
in 1952 and authorized by the National Council of Churches
of Christ in America which sponsored it. This new English,
or American, Bible will, if the Council can so persuade the
churches affiliated with it, replace the King James Version
issued in 1611 and the American Standard Version of 1901
for use in their pulpits, pews, and Sunday Schools. Among
National Council churches it is being vigorously promoted
in innumerable meetings and rallies.

It is the work of thirty-two of the foremost American

biblical scholars, headed by Luther A. Weigle of Yale University, who have been at the task since 1937; it has been reviewed by a council of cooperating denominations; and it has been so successfully promoted by its sponsors that in a few months it has overtopped the sale of any *new* book in American history and one must be put on a waiting list to obtain a copy.

The object of issuing this new version, which contains far more radical changes than the revision of 1901, is to replace words that have changed in meaning, or been lost in current use, with the language of today, while "preserving the beauty and simplicity of the King James Version." It must be judged by whether it accomplishes this. It has already created a considerable controversy, particularly among the more fundamentalist sects, not all of whose criticisms I share.

I do not believe that every dot, comma, and phrase of the King James Version is sacrosanct. How, indeed, could they be? The original Bible, Old and New Testaments, was written by many teachers, prophets, philosophers, bards, or historians over a period of some 900 years before and after Christ, some of it probably recited, as folk-poetry or folk-tales and recorded much later than the first words were uttered. Originally written in Hebrew, Greek, and Aramaic, it has undergone many translations, and no translation, if it be a great and fine one, is ever exactly literal. It has had numerous translations even into English, where it did not make its earliest European appearance. The first of these English versions were in manuscript, not printed form, and were all translations from the Latin Vulgate, itself a translation, and the earliest of them, which appeared in the seventh century, is largely incomprehensible today by anyone not a scholar of early English — far harder to understand than Chaucer, who wrote several centuries later.

The King James Version had, during less than a century, three predecessors, one of which, the version of William Tyndale, was translated directly from the Hebrew and Greek, almost contemporaneously with Martin Luther's great translation into German. Tyndale's was a noble work, for which its writer paid with his life, but in the King James Version the work was started all over again. This, the King James, was the first version *authorized* by ecclesiastical and state authorities for public and church use.

The King James Version has chapter and verse forms that appear arbitrary and confusing, and punctuation — especially a plethora of commas, colons, and semicolons — that hold up rather than guide the reader. Passages of poetry in scannable verse are printed as prose. Passages which clearly belong together are broken into separate chapters for no discernible reason, as are chapters into arbitrary verses. And the chronology of events is not always accurate, according to later researchers.

For this reason I welcomed *The Bible, Designed to Be Read as Living Literature* when it appeared in 1936, as arranged and edited by Ernest Sutherland Bates. Although not the whole Bible it is the noblest part of it, and it is so printed, arranged, and classified into sections as to carry along the eye and mind and not interrupt and divert them. But this Bible is in the exact words of the King James Version except for a minority of passages where the revision of 1901 is prefered. Passages which are clearly verse are so printed. In the new Bible that we are here discussing, verse passages are also put in a verse form of printing, but it is, to my eye and mind, an extremely awkward form, neither quite poetry nor prose, while the rhythms of the King James Version are badly marred by modernizing the speech.

The men in the reign of King James who produced the great Bible were a large body of the greatest scholars of the

period. They were headed by the greatest of them all, Dr.
Andrewes, later Bishop of Winchester, who was equally at
home in Hebrew, Aramaic, Syriac, and Greek. The fidelity
of their text to the original has never since been successfully
challenged, and its beauty makes it the greatest monument of
the English language, as Martin Luther's Bible is of the German. It appeared in an age when the Reformation was re-
vitalizing the religious sense of the people; in an age when
men had gone to the block for the right to print and read the
Bible; it coincided with the English renaissance that produced
Shakespeare; it was written when the English language was
most vivid and virile. All these factors combined to produce
the clarity, simplicity, passion, beauty, and majesty of the
King James Bible which has outlasted all subsequent revisions.

Therefore, whoever takes up this masterpiece with a
view to "bringing it up to date" or "putting it into modern
language" is, apart from theological considerations, running
the same risks that would face anyone who sat down to re-
write *Hamlet* or *King Lear* or any other work of a writer or
writers of genius, the more so because the English Bible, like
others, has contributed its phraseology and figures of speech
to the language, and therefore, though archaic, its words are
ever-living. The King James Version has also, in parts, been
put to music — in the great oratorios, and in Protestant
hymns. We no longer say "liveth." But we sing, "I know
that my Redeemer liveth," and we cannot substitute "lives"
without losing a beat of the music. And apart from musical
accompaniment, this matter of beat, cadence, the rise and
fall of sentences is part of the magic of poetry or prose, contributing to its evocative character, its overtones and under-
tones, its symphonic style, which greatly distinguishes the
familiar Bible.

I have tried to read the new Bible of the American scholars
with an open mind, and without prejudice, indeed with

humility and with respect for so great an effort. Perhaps this is not entirely possible for one so wedded to a familiar text. But I am compelled to say that I find the new text inferior on nearly every page to the one it seeks to supplant, and for reasons which I think I can define. It is weaker, less vivid, defective in imagery, less beautiful, and less inspired. And I, at least, do not find it easier to understand.

As an example of the weakening of the old text, take the 42nd Psalm:

> As the hart panteth after the water brooks,
> So panteth my soul after thee, O God.
> My soul thirsteth for God, for the living God: . . .

In the new version we read:

> As the hart longs
>   for flowing streams,
> So longs my soul
>   for thee, O God.
> My soul thirsts for God,
>   for the living God. . . .

In the King James Version we see and hear the panting hart. The image of the stag comes immediately to mind. He is running, searching for water, until he is out of breath, his breath heaves in gasps, his tongue protrudes. His thirst is desperate and urgent and the simile of thirst is vivid: My need of God is like the thirst of the stag, who, if he does not find the brook of water will surely die.

In the new version this sense of action and urgency is gone. The hart merely "longs" for water with no visible effects of the lack of it. And no picture of a "longing" stag can be invoked. Longing is in the mind, not the flesh, and how do I know that a stag has a mind to long? Is he just sitting in the underbrush vaguely hoping? What *sign* is there of his thirst, to which the thirst of the human soul after God can be compared?

Read both passages aloud for the beat and fall of the words. The King James Version of the three lines falls in beats: 11-10-11 to a line. The cadence is poetry. That of the new version is prosaic.

For the authenticity of the one or the other as a translation I cannot vouch, because I know no Hebrew. But it must, I think, have conveyed some idea of urgency physically expressed, for the Luther Bible, also translated from the originals, conveys this. In the German text the animal *schreit* after the water streams — i.e., howls, shrieks, gives voice to loud cries, as, in the next line, does the soul after God. Luther used the strongest verb in the German language to convey the painful cry of urgency. Does this seem quibbling? I think not. I think it goes to the very root of effective writing.

The new version is altogether less robust. In Job 15 the King James Version makes Job say, "Should a wise man make answer with vain knowledge, and fill his belly with the east wind?" The new version says, "Should a wise man answer with windy knowledge, and fill himself with the east wind?"

What is this a concession to? Some prissiness? The Bible, especially the Old Testament is not at all squeamish about the body and prefers the specific and precise to the general. "Vain knowledge" is futile knowledge; windy knowledge is no knowledge at all. And it is wind in the belly and not anywhere else that causes discomfort and embarrassment. And the belly (*Bauch*) is in Luther's Bible, too.

I cannot understand at all certain changes. In the familiar Isaian prophecy (53:5) are the words:

"But he was wounded for our transgressions, he was bruised for our iniquities: the chastisement of our peace was upon him; and with his stripes we are healed."

This passage, of incomparable poetic flow, is marred to my ears by the change of the phrase "the chastisement of our peace" to the cumbersome "Upon him was the chastisement that made us whole." I confess I do not know what that means, except the chastisement that healed us, which is a repetition, then, of the next line, "and with his stripes we are healed." Is there no mention of our peace in the original? There is in the Luther Bible.

Throughout the new text I look for words graven in my memory and do not find them. The "whited sepulcher" that every literate person knows as a symbol of gilded corruption is, in the new version, a "whitewashed tomb." This does not modernize the phrase, for a whitewashed tomb is no nearer to our present experience than the other phrase. And what more manly and robust expression of unshakable faith than Job's words (Chapter 13), "Though he slay me, yet will I trust in him."? How many people in the 342 years since the great English Bible appeared have not spoken those words silently to themselves through rebellious years? But you will not find them in the new Bible which reads, "Behold, he will slay me; I have no hope."

Nor can I understand other changes from the viewpoint of improved simplicity and clarity. The King James Version of the Twenty-seventh Psalm reads:

> *The Lord is my light and my salvation; whom shall I fear? the Lord is the strength of my life; of whom shall I be afraid?*

The new version changes "strength" to "stronghold," marring the cadence, and to what purpose? We speak of the strength of the arm, of the heart, of the life. Why encompass pulsing life in a fortress? Surely not for the sake of a more simple expression! Again, in the same psalm, "When the wicked, even mine enemies and my foes, came upon me to eat up my flesh, they stumbled and fell," is changed to "When evildoers assail me, uttering slanders against me, my adversaries and foes, they shall stumble and fall."

Why "evildoers," an awkward word in the context and not so forthright as "wicked"? Why change of tense?

Again, in the famous passage in Matthew 7 about the mote in one's brother's eye and the beam in one's own, "mote" becomes "speck" and "beam" "log." Neither mote nor beam is an obsolete word; the long vowel in each is pleasant to the ear and the phrase "the mote and the beam" has become part of the vocabulary of every well-read person.

So has the expression "many mansions" — "In my father's house are many mansions." Granted that the word "house" is more circumvented in current usage than it was at the beginning of the seventeenth century when it could be synonymous with "household," the new version which reads "In my father's house are many rooms" removes the stately and palatial concept of the old version. My "father's house" is the house of a King, not a boardinghouse or the cubicles of a Y.M.C.A. The word "home" may include more than four walls and a roof. We use it to describe a great estate, or even a whole country. "In my father's *home* are many mansions" would remove the apparent contradiction in the old text, while keeping the picture, the familiar phrase, and the identical rhythm.

The mere presence or elision of a comma can be disturbing to one who knows the Bible. Few passages from the King James Version are better known than the vision of Isaiah (9:2), the passage beginning, "The people that walked in darkness have seen a great light" — interpreted as a prophecy of the coming of the Messiah — whose "name shall be called

Wonderful, Counsellor, The Mighty God, The Everlasting Father, The Prince of Peace."

The new version omits the comma after "Wonderful," so that passage reads, "Wonderful Counsellor." This is a trivial use of the word wonderful with its content of marvel, supernatural, inexplicable. Surely the King James translators, like Luther, set the word apart for a reason. His name shall be called "the Wonderful." As an adjective modifying "Counsellor" it is ill-chosen. A counsellor can be just, wise, excellent, but hardly wondrous, or wonderful.

I find over and over again in this new version what appear to me as unhappy substitutions of words. In Matthew 5 (the Beatitudes) instead of the traditional opening, "And seeing the multitudes, he went up into a mountain: and when he was set, his disciples came unto him: And he opened his mouth, and taught them, saying . . .", we read the substitute phrase, "Seeing the crowds . . ." But "crowds" is not a substitute for "multitudes," a word connoting numbers of people gathered together as individuals. A crowd is a collective entity, in which the person is submerged. The *New Oxford Dictionary* defines a crowd as "a number of persons gathered so closely together as to press each other" and the sense of the crowd is immediately communicated when the noun is used as a verb, where it means to push, shove, press — "Don't *crowd* me." Luther's Bible describes the gathering simply as "the people" (*volk*).

There is insufficient space in a brief commentary such as this one to pile illustration upon illustration as could be done, but as one final example of what seems to me to be emasculation of language there is the changed version of the Thirteenth Chapter of First Corinthians, beginning, "Though I speak with the tongues of men and of angels, and have not charity . . ." This little essay of only 272 words has always seemed to me to be one of the most perfect passages of prose in our language, the content and form so perfectly wedded that I cannot see how anyone would dare to touch it.

Previous, as well as later, versions substituted the word "love" for "charity." Luther used it (*Liebe*) in the first place. "Charity" has, alas, lost much of its content of cherishing and Christian lovingkindness. "Love" no doubt is closer to the original meaning. But I do not see why the new authors chose to begin with " 'If' I speak," instead of with "Though I speak . . ." — for "though" suggests that I may well be able to speak like an angel and is closer to the sense of what follows, while "if" is more indifferently conditional, and "though," with its long round vowel is a word of greater tone than the iffy "if."

What follows the though's, or the if's, is a description of what Christian and loving behavior is not and is; what it does not and does *do*. I underline "do" because throughout the chapter verbs are used, eight of them in as many lines: "Charity suffereth long . . . envieth not . . . vaunteth not itself, is not puffed up, Doth not behave itself unseemly, seeketh not her own . . . thinketh no evil; Rejoiceth not in iniquity, but rejoiceth in the truth."

Now verbs, the words of action, are the strongest category of words in the language, and great and strong writing avoids adjectives and adverbs as enemies that weaken nouns and verbs. The soliloquy of Hamlet, almost all nouns and verbs, is an example. But whereas the King James Version expresses love and the antithesis of loving behavior in eight lines containing eight verbs and only two adjectives, the new version uses seven adjectives and only two verbs. Love no longer suffereth long but is "patient." "Love" — the new version continues — "is not jealous or boastful; it is not arrogant or rude . . . irritable or resentful." If these are adequate substitutes for, or an improvement upon, the old version in which the unloving are *behaving* themselves, actively, in unpleasant ways, then all that I have tried to learn about writing the English language in a generation of effort has been wasted. And, unquestionably, the exquisite balance and rhythm of the chapter, which thousands of people have committed to memory, is injured.

Probably in the long run, this will not matter. The new Bible may, indeed, awaken a fresh interest in the Bible, and lead many to read it, even to read the King James Version. Had I no other Bible, I would read this one, for it, too, is the Great Book.

But I would always hear as an overtone to its flatter, if more modern speech the distant thunder and the majestic music of the old.

Beware of Geniuses!

IT HAS BEEN my fate during much of my life to be mixed up in one way or another with geniuses. I don't know what there is about me that attracts them. They see me coming. They spot me a mile off.

It is not because they feel me to be a kindred spirit touched with a spark of their sacred fire. Quite the contrary. They believe me to be an antidote for their afflictions; an antibiotic to bring down their fevers or a cheery hot water bottle for a chill. They have never called me their inspiration. They have never swum the Hellespont for me. My business has been to be on hand with hot grog and aspirin after the plunge.

I am the bread and milk, never the caviar. I am the pickup, never the wine. I am not the subject of an ode but the object. They must come around and read it to me at 3 A.M. I do not inflict their wounds. I am the bandage. I am not the lightning. I am the lightning rod.

Geniuses have gravitated to me regardless of age, sex, or nationality. I remind them of their mothers. They may be years older than I, but it makes no difference. I am always the older. This gave me prematurely gray hair. I was cast for the role of Whistler's mother before I was thirty.

All in all, I have in my life been closely associated with five geniuses for shorter or longer periods of time. I say they were geniuses because the world (or discriminating people) thought them so, and they themselves had no doubt about it. Maybe they were not great geniuses. Time, I think, is the only test of that. But they met one or another of the descriptions or definitions of genius that have been made many times. Agatha Young has assembled some of these definitions in *Scalpel*, a collection of brief biographies of history's way-breaking surgeons. Diderot believed that genius depends on enthusiasm and deep emotion; Matthew Arnold, that it is largely a matter of energy; the Abbé Du Bois (in 1775), that it "consists of a happy arrangement of the organs." With some interpretation, all these definitions apply. Enthusiasm, emotion, and energy, not diffused but intensely if sporadically concentrated, characterized them all. If the good Abbé meant that the physical structure of the brain is involved, I would be inclined to agree. Thomas Carlyle defined genius as "the transcendent capacity for taking trouble" (usually quoted as "taking pains"). I always read that dictum as "the capacity for *making* trouble" — for conventional minds and for their associates. They always made trouble for me.

My attraction for geniuses, although maddening, requires some explanation of myself, for I went on welcoming it for a long time, even after I should have known better. It is a horrid snobbish thought, but fame *does* attract most people, and although not all of them were famous when I met them first, they all had something about them which made me sure they would or should be. In every case I immensely admired their work, recognizing its originality. Geniuses are never imitative. Admiring their work, I was flattered by the thought that I might be, in some way, contributing to it even if only by offering a hot meal to the poet, playright, novelist, or painter. (I should say right here that the geniuses who have passed in and out of my life have never been philosophers or scientists, but always imaginative creative artists of one sort or another.)

And they were fascinating — when they were not excruciatingly boring. Nobody can be both to such a high or low degree as a genius. They are always up or down. Being the knitted comforter, I got them oftenest when they were down.

But, since I early discovered that geniuses are not like other boys and girls, I was also moved by curiosity. I wanted to find out what made them tick. I never did. Some have passed on and books have been written about them, recounting in the most intimate detail the circumstances of their lives and analyzing them with the benefit of Freud, Jung, or Adler, but I have never read a book about a genius I have known that seemed to me to be exactly true. Something was always left out, and something extraneous, revelatory not of the genius but of the author, was always put in. I have been besieged with questions from biographers of geniuses. How did he (or she) feel about his parents? Who (or what) was the decisive influence in his life? And many more intimate questions. The biographers have thought me mean or secretive when I said I didn't know. But it was an honest answer.

Not that I had not been the recipient of confidences! And how! I have heard enough confessions and soul searchings to rate a psychoanalyst's license. But not being a psychoanalyst, I was never able to spot fact from fancy. For this is a thing about geniuses. By any usual (or normal) standards they are colossal liars. They are not *conscious* liars. They absolutely believe that what they are telling you is true, even if it is not remotely like what they told you a week before about the same relationship or event. Every experience relived in their imaginations undergoes a sea change into something so rich and strange that nobody who has shared the experience could possibly recognize it.

There is no good in arguing with geniuses about such matters of fact; and if you did, you would probably, in a supersensory realm that you cannot penetrate, be wrong. Every genius I have known had powers of association too vast and complex for me to follow. A thing, an image, an event, an idea would ray out in all directions, associate and reassociate with myriads of other things, images, events, and ideas, to come to rest in a new pattern. The mind structure of geniuses seems different from that of other people, even other formidably intelligent people. The kind of intelligence a genius has is a different sort of intelligence. The thinking of a genius does not proceed logically. It leaps with great ellipses. It pulls knowledge from God knows where.

A genius who knew absolutely nothing about economics and rarely read a newspaper looked into the street from his publisher's office on Madison Avenue an hour after landing in America after a long absence and said, "Within a year this country will have a terrible financial panic." In answer to the obvious question of why he thought so, he replied impatiently, "I don't think. I know. Can't you *see* it, *smell* it? I can *see* people jumping out of windows on this very street."

Within a year the crash came — and when reminded, he could not recall his prediction at all. This is not an isolated case. Maybe, in addition to a peculiar brain structure, geniuses also have superior radio-receiving stations. Two I have known (a woman and a man) were capable of living simultaneously in various times, whereby something that may have happened a thousand years ago was occurring right now. Not that something now *resembled* or *recalled* an ancient occurrence. It was the *same* occurrence in their minds. That is why it is quite hard at times to distinguish a genius from a lunatic. Indeed, many geniuses would be so certified if what they created did not contradict the doctor. Yet these people of whom I have spoken exercised in large areas of their lives normal common sense.

But for ordinary living, it is well to take everything a genius tells you with a large grain of salt. Not all they "see" materializes. What seems like clairvoyance may be real clairvoyance (for want of a better word) or it may merely be a passing fancy.

As for human relationships, the genius' account of them is also likely to be strictly unreliable. If he tells you he had an overbearing father and a cruel stepmother, do not let it bother you too much. If he is a writer, remember he is by profession a storyteller. If he recounts an extraordinary experience in the heart of Africa, enjoy the story, but do not accept it as accurate reporting. If a lady genius tells you she is going to commit suicide that very night because of unrequited love, think twice before you warn the police.

For, in my experience, geniuses are very tough. They are more likely to drive others to suicide than commit it themselves — unless there is a far more compelling reason than "love." A genius is obsessed by three fears, none of which is fear of losing a loved one. These are, first and last, the fear (or realization) of losing his (or her) creative powers; the fear (or realization) of losing his mind — which sometimes occurs; and (sometimes) the fear of never gaining, or of losing, his public. There have been geniuses who could live for years without recognition or applause, but once they have won it, they feed upon it.

All the geniuses I have known have been immensely egotistic. A "sacred" egotism I am prepared to concede. Those of them who have worked for years without any recognition, their desks filled with rejected manuscripts or their studios stacked with rejected pictures, have been sustained by this egotism. It seems as though by mystery a fairy godmother touched the child in his cradle, printing upon his forehead an invisible star, setting him off for ever from other people as possessing a talent unique to himself, and inimitable.

He may discover it in childhood, but he is more likely first to discover merely that he is not like other boys or girls, is disliked by his playmates, and is thoroughly miserable. This is probably why the geniuses I have known — and however much they may later have "overcompensated" — have been painfully shy. Apart from their parents, their first contacts were with other children, and children in general are cruel conformists.

The genius may discover his gift in early maturity, or come to recognize it initially only through its recognition by others.

But once he knows that he has it, its guardianship and enhancement are the *only* matters of consequence in his life. It is embodied in himself and he is, literally, its incarnation.

This affects his attitudes toward conventional morality. Whatever is good for him as an artist is good per se, and he alone is the judge. If a passionate love affair stimulates a poem, a picture, a drama, or a novel, it is good — for that purpose. When its purpose is exhausted, it is no longer good and that it involves another human being is, at most, regrettable. If alcohol or drugs temporarily fire a waning imagination he will indulge in them, or he may seek them as an anodyne during an uncreative period. But if ever convinced that they will be the death of him (he being the repository of the gift) he may stop the fatal habit from one day to another.

I do not here suggest that all geniuses are dissolute. None of them is dissolute all the time. A genius, also, may be by conventional standards a prig. George Bernard Shaw refrained from alcohol, tobacco, and meat, was given to lecturing others on these three vices, and his latest biographer claims that he became a married celibate at thirty-five. The point is that however he argued it, he created the conditions essential to his work. If immoderation in anything is a vice, his work was a vice.

If you are the close friend of a genius, you will soon learn that nothing matters to him except creative work, and that he feels but one responsibility — to answer at the Last Judgment for what he has done with his unique talent. Whatever his other vices, in this he is formidably moral. He will starve and let his wife and children starve rather than debase that talent. He will sweat and bleed and all but die for one page of words on paper or a square foot of paint on canvas, and expect meanwhile to be waited on hand and foot, and by deaf mutes. Never interrupt an artist in the middle of his work! You are inflicting agony upon him.

However disorderly the rest of their lives may be, geniuses are meticulous in their work. It is never, never, never *quite* good enough — not for others, but for themselves. They respect no other critics.

The geniuses I have known have been very odd about money. Artists who earn their living by their work are often sure, no matter how much money they may be making or have in the bank, that they will end in the poorhouse. That is because they are forever haunted by the fear that they cannot keep on doing it — the miraculous thing — and usually, after an intense creative period, that they are finished for ever. The intensity with which a genius works is like no other intensity. He (or she) will forget to eat, forget to go to bed, forget to wake up, forget the invitation he has accepted — and rage that it has been accepted in his behalf, even when he phoned and did it himself. He will rise at four in the morning and sleep at four in the afternoon, or he may suddenly settle down and work from nine to five like a bureaucrat. At times during his work he will have to test it on an audience. He will want to know exactly what you think of it. No matter what you think, say it is undoubtedly going to be the best work of his life. For an adverse criticism, however justified, will send him into the doldrums and have not the slightest effect. The only person a genius is really trying to satisfy is himself, and he always knows whether his work is good or mediocre or plain bad. He only hopes other critics, less severe than he, will not find it out. If you confirm his worst fears he will hate you, himself, and everything around him. He is losing his gift, he will storm, because the baby cries, or his wife plays the piano, or the housemaid gave him an odd look, or critics are dolts, or the times are out of joint, or the sun is shining, or it's raining, or he had an unhappy childhood, or his parents spoiled him, or because (with a fortune in his bank account) he is being driven by the need for money to writing trash to pay for the new Cadillac.

Do not let any of this disturb you. He can't help it. It isn't a fact — but don't argue.

However, there may come a moment when you, as his dearest friend, or wife (or husband) will drive him even more frantic by your equanimity. He will demand that you share his sufferings, and agree that he is surrounded by knaves, fools, sycophants, by a gigantic conspiracy involving nature and even God Almighty to ruin his gift. You must participate in his rage.

That is where you are all but certain to break down. Because if you begin to share that rage which is his, not yours, you will soon suspect that *you* are going crazy. Since geniuses are extremely persuasive, you may indeed be carried along into the rage, but always with a nagging mental reservation and a bad hangover of remorse. He won't have a hangover. If he gets a fresh new start on his picture, his novel, his play, if what he creates next day pleases him, then the whole world will be beautiful again.

Money, like everything else, must serve to enhance his gift, embodied in himself. The genius, though he fears to end his days in poverty, can be sour about the household bills, declare that the servants are lazy and overpaid, and decide simultaneously to take the family on an African safari, rent another house in the country, and fly de luxe around the world. His gift isn't being fed and replenished by the well-conducted household and by the devoted and by no means overpaid servants. The spark of genius, he thinks, needs higher-powered fuel to make it flame.

A very great lady poet whose works revealed high humaneness sided with a dull and selfish woman who bought perfumes at $60 an ounce, and thought $60 a high enough monthly wage for any cook. (You've guessed! This was prewar.) A woman like myself thought there was a strange disparity of values here. But the poet cried, "Ah, but she is right. A cook is a cook. But a scent — that awakens the imagination. A scent is a dream."

How does anyone know that that was not "true"? The lady genius loved to cook when she was in a mood for it, but when in a frenzy of work neither knew nor cared what she ate or whether she ate at all. An apple, a sandwich, a glass of milk would do. But her dressing table was an exotic garden.

Geniuses are, again by conventional standards, monstrously selfish. There is a theory, supported by some cases, that geniuses do not care how they look. That has not been my experience. Male or female, they like to deck themselves in fine raiment, often regardless of the clothes budget of the rest of the family; and are painfully conscious of any physical flaws in themselves. They want the gift to be suitably enshrined.

If in the sustenance of the gift they are extravagant, they are otherwise stingy. They know what the work they have produced has cost — the tax to the limit, and sometimes beyond the limit, the ecstasy of some moments, the awful emptiness of others. For the expenditure of such mental and emotional effort, fame and money are the only external rewards. They want the money they have earned; haggle with publishers or dealers, challenge agents, rage that they must pay income tax, demand preposterous payments and fees, seeing in all with whom they have financial relations only parasites living off their unique, inimitable gift, of which every work represents another painful birth.

"Why should I go through all this?" they cry. "For others to garner its fruits?" Of course, they have to "go through all this," fruits or no fruits. They are commanded and compelled. They are possessed.

For their most intimate friends, and especially for their wives, or their husbands, there invariably comes a painful awakening. That is the moment when one realizes that one is entirely dispensable. The genius creates in everyone he brings closest to him the illusion (an illusion undoubtedly, if temporarily, shared by himself) that that person is indispensable. And there is no bond stronger than the bond of indispensability, the notion that "without me, he will die, or become unable to create."

But nobody is indispensable to a genius. *Nobody*. Indispensable to genius is only its own demon, and that demon's needs. Unrequited love may nurture it and requited love stifle it. "I loved a woman and my love was not returned, but out of it I have written these songs," said Walt Whitman. A heartbreak that can be sublimated into a work of art is no heartbreak. It is only another transforming experience, from which a genius will arise again, "with a song from the reedy shallows" — with other friends, other loves, and other heartbreaks.

But when the demon, the great gift, deserts the genius — when the inimitable begins imitating himself; when the critics lament and he, in his heart, silently agrees; when the euphoric ecstasy of the creative moment is gone and his work becomes merely able craftsmanship; when the gift has drifted out and quietly closed the door — comes the heartbreak that kills.

In general, therefore, I would advise those susceptible to genius to walk promptly away before too hopelessly smitten. And above all not to let it become a habit.

If a genius proposes to you, change your address and take your name out of the telephone book, or, if you can afford it, take a plane to another continent and live under an assumed name until his madness (and yours) is over. Recognize that you are no genius yourself, and that genius is better understood upon reflection, and from a distance.

You might, in your lengthening days, get a book out of the genius or geniuses you have known, loved, or thought you nurtured with your ministrations. But it will not be a "definitive" biography — if a definitive biography was ever written about a genius. For that you would have to know what you do not know, remember everything, forget nothing except yourself, be in possession of scholarly detachment and a deeply loving and illuminated understanding, without resentment, self-defense, or an impulse to reopen old arguments. That is a nonexistent combination even in a genius.

The best you can possibly get out of loving association with a genius or geniuses, is, at long length, a sobless tear, a chuckle of laughter, a pity that no longer excruciates, wider insights than you would otherwise have had, and a robust unweakened conviction that on balance genius more than pays its way in the world, even though it has a transcendent capacity for making trouble.

The World of Grandma Moses

THERE IS A LAW in life and nature that works infallibly. It is that everything must be paid for. Every loss brings some gain; every gain entails a loss. For everything one desires something that one also cherishes must be exchanged.

There is no such thing in human affairs as infinite progress, the illusion of the last century out of which has grown most of the "isms" and "ideologies" of the past hundred years. All of them are Messianic in that they promise the evolution of man into a perfect state of bliss, denying the compensatory forces that forever operate.

The paintings of Grandma Moses and their extraordinary popularity seem to me to illustrate this. The painter herself is a phenomenon. Never having painted seriously until she was seventy-seven, and having had no formal training whatever, the pictures of this farm woman, whose life since childhood has been one of hard toil, have captured the critics, enchanted the public, and made her at ninety-six, and from her own standards at least, a rich woman.

Being hailed by the critics as an "authentic American primitive" has boosted the prices of her pictures and attracted those buyers who look at all purchases of art as an investment that will retain or increase its money value. But there is no money value in the reproductions that others buy and live with so pleasurably.

She is not a great artist, whose hallmark is always intensity and originality of expression, rising above but grounded upon superb craftsmanship. She lacks their power to disturb, or elicit wonder, or evoke in the beholder a new and distinguished experience. What, then, accounts for her fame? Is it not that she illustrates a world that has gone beyond hope of recovery, and that in restrospect wears the aura of a lost paradise?

Is the view wholly sentimental?

Grandma Moses depicts — and idealizes — scenes from the upstate New York farming community where she still lives as she recalls them from her childhood and youth. What distinguishes them is freedom, gaiety, and boundless and diverse activity, going on without the pressures of mechanical time.

But how was life actually conducted?

It was a life of "back-breaking" toil, almost totally without "labor-saving" devices. The horse power of the farm was horses, mules, or oxen whom the farmer followed with his plow, harrow, and reaper. Fuel was cut in the woodlot with an axe (not a powered chain saw) and split or sawed by hand in the woodshed. Homes were heated with chunk stoves, requiring stoking, and food was cooked and water heated on a wood-burning range. Laundry was washed on a scrub board with homemade soap made of leftover fats, soda, and lye, and pressed with irons heated on the stove. Children attended ungraded school irregularly, seldom went beyond "grammar" school and often left to work with their fathers after the fifth or sixth grade, though there were exceptions — youngsters who went on to "academies" and farther, as the biographies of many great Americans attest, but even then "working their way through."

Families were large, but many children died early from diseases and epidemics not even diagnosed — or children lost one or another of their parents from "black" fever, "inflammation of the bowels" (probably appendicitis), "brain fever" — meningitis? — and from typhoid and diphtheria. But that was not only true on farms.

The farm was a hive of industry, in which everyone participated, including very small children.

There were always cattle and poultry to feed, vegetables to hoe, wood to split, lamps to be cleaned and filled, clothes to be cut, sewed, made over, patched, and darned. Berries had to be picked, apples gathered, butter churned, vegetables and fruit pickled, jellied, or canned in Mason jars, and meat salted, smoked, corned, or also canned. Long shelves crowded with jars hung from the rafters of deep cellars along with bacon and hams. Barrels and great stone jars held salt pork, corned beef, pickled beets, cucumbers, apples. There were gunny sacks full of dried beans, carrots and other vegetables in boxes of sand, and always a huge bin of potatoes.

These cellars were really "stores," holding most of the edibles one can buy in stores today, as well as preserves, pickles, and relishes, the recipes for which are hard to find today. And all this autumn to autumn store was grown and processed by the family itself.

As a child and young girl whose father was a minister in upstate New York in villages surrounded by farms, I often visited the farm homes of his parishioners and once lived with one of them for several months. My recollection is of amazing abundance, of breakfasts that would be other people's dinners and dinners that would be others' banquets. Not *one* dessert, but pie *and* cake, cookies and doughnuts, following meat, potatoes or a huge platter of eggs and an array of vegetables, with pickles on the side. Homemade bread fresh every day, popovers, muffins, gems fresh from the oven, and all consumed with the gargantuan appetites of those continually in fresh air and on the move. I was "allowed" to collect eggs, pick and shell peas, gather strawberries and raspberries, make beds, and ride the farm horses, all of which seemed to me, working with other boys and girls, the most superior form of play I had ever known.

Sleeping rooms then were "chambers," their beds covered with "comforters," quilted in tiny stitches by hand, atop feather beds, their tickings stuffed with the more downy feathers of the farm's slaughtered poultry. And if the rooms were chilly, so much cozier the beds.

The kitchen, invariably the largest, brightest room in the house, was the center of family life, parlor or sitting room being open only for visitors. There was the iron or soapstone sink and the hand pump that brought water from the spring — where milk was also cooled. Here stood the foot-treadled sewing machine and the mending basket, the big table at which everybody ate the enormous early breakfasts, noon dinners, and simple suppers.

"Everybody" usually included a widowed aunt, a parentless nephew, niece, or cousin, and the hired man, a homeless widower, perhaps, or the strapping son of another farmer, with more sons than he needed or could feed at home. They did not work for wages beyond pocket money. They shared a home. Grandmother, or sometimes great-grandmother, was often there too, ensconced in a rocking chair, too old to do much but putter a little, wash dishes, peel vegetables, and tell stories to the children.

For this was another characteristic of the world of Grandma Moses. There was always room for one more. When original accommodations were exhausted the menfolks took timber to the sawmill, traded it for sawed boards and siding, built another chamber, added an ell to the kitchen, broke a dormer into the attic, and finished off a plastered room, mixing the sand, lime, and water plaster themselves, so that the odd dormers and irregular juts of many old farmhouses record the growth of the family.

Who wants to live like that today?

Nobody does, and few, if any, could. But we are speaking of compensations — of the fact that with every gain something is lost.

The world of Grandma Moses was a world of free men, free in the sense of being independent, autonomous in themselves and able by themselves and with their families to meet every family need.

The land on which they lived, their homes, farms, and animals were their own, and what they produced was sufficient for themselves, sufficient to share with others and to trade for the little else they needed. They were almost completely divorced from a money economy and the need of money.

In Vermont, where I have lived for four months every year for nearly a generation, I have friends, older men and women, who lived the earlier part of their lives just that way. Some of them are living on the farms to which they went as brides or grooms thirty or forty years ago. But they are not the *same* farms, nor are they surrounded by other farms or their old neighbors. One of them recently recalled that when she married thirty-eight years ago the farming community on the road-connected hills where her home stands numbered twenty-two households, all with large families, so that there were four one-room schools. Now only five families still hold on, elderly people, their children married or gone into other occupations. There is no school. There are no children to attend one.

What has happened to those farms? Two or three have been sold to "summer folks," for our town is very beautiful, with a salubrious summer climate and matchless autumns and Indian summers. These houses have been remodeled, but their land is returning to the wilderness out of which it was hewed, its crumbling stone walls reminding one of the infinitude of labor, individual and communal, that built them out of the stones of the fields that, like the forests, had to be cleared.

A great tract of them has been bought by a university that is timbering and reforesting it to afford the institution a perpetual income. But it no longer provides livelihoods for robust families.

The same story applies to the whole county, which, as far as the quality of land is concerned, is one of the better counties in the state. But the farm population has been dwindling year by year. In 1880 this county had 35,196 inhabitants and 4455 farms. In 1954 its population just topped 40,000, but there were only 1609 farms. Farm acreage had been reduced from 420,099 acres to 324,152, despite the increased size of the farms still operating. One man produces, with his machines, more per acre than his 1880 predecessors but farming as a way of life has radically declined.

There are still family farms but the old economy is gone. The better homes are far more comfortable than the ones I

have described. They have electric lights, mechanical refrig-
eration, bathrooms, freezers, radios, television sets. In the
barns are milking machines and sometimes mechanical feeders,
and in the sheds stand tractors and hay balers, which have
replaced the old draft animals.

Diversity of operation has given way to concentration.
Instead of four or five cows, the farmer must have thirty,
forty, or preferably more to bring him in an adequate milk
check, and their production must be copious and high in
butter fat, requiring heavy grain feeding and high-protein
hay. The farmer cannot afford to "waste his time" on a large
vegetable garden. He must concentrate on his money crop,
because, unlike his father and grandfather, he is perpetually
in need of money.

His father could buy a good team of horses for $350 and
they reproduced themselves, with a surplus of colts to sell,
and provided fertilizer for his fields. They and their progeny
never wore out or needed new spare parts. They were an
inexhaustible capital. Now, this farmer's son has twenty
thousand dollars or more invested in machinery whose lifetime is not likely to be more than five years before it is turned
in, greatly below the original price.

The machinery consumes gas and oil, which the farmer
cannot grow but must buy. It produces inadequate natural
fertilizer for his need for high field production. This compels
him to purchase commercial fertilizers, a recurrent annual
expenditure that for a two-hundred-acre farm will easily
cost him $1000. He drives the land and is, in turn, driven
by it, and there are champions of organic farming who believe the land is already taking its revenge.

He is controlled by inspectors who can, at any moment,
bar his milk from the market — if the cooler is not more than
an exact number of feet from the milk barn, or if the elec-

tricity goes off in the cooler, or if the manure is allowed to accumulate more than a certain length of time (and what does one do if it is impossible, because of weather, to spread it on the fields?). The milk will not be accepted in any case if the bacteria count fails to meet requirements, so he wonders just why his every step must be ordered for him.

If the price of milk, or any other product he grows, falls in relation to what he must buy, he is caught in the "cost-price" squeeze and bankruptcy looms. It is wonderful for his wife to have an electric or gas range, a washing machine, lots of hot water, and an automatic furnace, but the installations are expensive and there is a monthly bill for them, whereas the fuel from the woodlot costs nothing in cash.

He cannot "trade in" his products at the local stores. They have their own suppliers and deal largely in packaged goods. He cannot retail his richly creamy milk to the villagers. Anyone can pasteurize milk at home, but to sell it retail the farmer must put up a pasteurizing-homogenizing plant, whose price a medium-sized farm can never earn.

To get the largest possible cash income from his investments, the small farmer often "hires himself out," together with his machinery, digging ponds for large estates and working on the public roads. Often his wife or daughters work out too. For the new home equipment must also be paid for and maintained. The farmer cannot say, as his father did, "No wife of mine will ever work for strangers."

The notion that mechanization is "labor saving" thus proves illusory. In the over-all sense it is obviously so. Technology consumes labor voraciously, creating more and more "jobs." But it is illusory in the more intimate sense. On the farm it saves "labor" only by substituting manpower. The farmer himself works no shorter or less strenuous hours. He does not have more "time." On the contrary he is driven as never before to "make money."

Into the technical progress that his farm represents enters, therefore, an element of pressure and anxiety that was not there in the world of Grandma Moses. The old self-sufficient farmer, who grew to feed his family and animals abundantly, locally marketing and trading in the surplus, was rich by virtue of the modesty of his external needs. If he had a bumper crop and much surplus it was a jubilee year. But whether the farm yielded more or less was not a matter of life or death. It meant that Mary wouldn't have a new dress that year or Harry a new suit. It did not mean calamity. Now it can mean just that. For the new farmer is part of the enormous apparatus created by technology which enters every phase of production and distribution. In fact, he is not a farmer in the ancient sense of the word. He is a businessman. He must study the market, keep books on every cow and hen, and pay ever-increasing taxes even on his personal property, his cattle, and equipment. For in the motor age, roads that could be negotiated by horses defy a jeep. The needs of the community perpetually increase.

The community of closely knitted families is also breaking up. Its sons, even if they still live at home, go off to work in factories, sometimes forty miles away, for the high wages with which only the richest farmers can compete. Its daughters are no longer amused by grange dances, church festivals, and village picnics. They train themselves as stenographers, nurses, or bookkeepers, and go to the larger towns, or, if untrained, they work in the town's shops and stores, delight in the movies, and marry boys from the town. Their parents seldom have the joy of seeing their grown children and their grandchildren at the family board, and being able to say of the son-in-law, "Your dad was my best friend," or of the daughter-in-law, "You were a cute kid." The families are scattered, the in-laws are strangers, the village is a diminishing suburb of a larger town, and the drift is from village to town to city, from where the life of the village and farm, the products they buy, the markets they supply, and the conditions of their work are ever increasingly controlled.

Few wish to change this and none who do can. The great technological revolution has brought a vast increase of material consumption. But it has brought neither greater freedom nor security nor inner satisfaction.

Its inexorable trend is to collectivize and control the whole of economic and social life. It weeds out the "incompetent," meaning those incompetent to adjust to its demands. For autonomous man, the man whole in himself, it has no use. Its ideal is the perfectly functioning machine, in which the parts (though they be men and not pieces of steel) are subservient to the whole operation and the operation sufficient unto its own purpose. Its promise is an ever greater shower of goods to be consumed — and goods that *must* be consumed if the process is not to break down. It fulfills this promise but only at a price.

The price is the world of Grandma Moses: free, laborious, poor, but yet abundant.

On Children

I Remember Me

THE QUESTION of why children behave as they do provokes much public discussion involving criticism of parents and "family patterns," teachers and schools, with nowadays plentiful contributions by psychoanalysts, psychiatrists, and psychologists of every variety.

A forum panel recently debated the question "What creates hostility in children?" The answers included, as one might expect, emotional disturbances in the home, overdemands on the young, favoritism shown one child over another, the insecure conditions of the times, and other wise observations. What I missed, however, was the simple statement that what creates hostility in children is — childhood.

Children are *naturally* hostile; hostile to other children, in their own family and outside it; hostile to adults, including their own parents — and no matter how good, kind, and wise in the rearing of their young ones the parents may be. Little boys are belligerently aggressive and fight each other at the drop of a hat, for no apparent reason at all. Little girls quarrel violently, taking their dolls and going home in a high dudgeon or in angry tears. All normal children (or all I have ever known) regard adults in general as natural enemies, to which there may be occasional or temporary exceptions. Grownups are persons who can do things not allowed to children. Or grownups do things children think absurd. Grownups often seem *stupid* to a child. Worst of all, grownups are Authority.

Probably the greatest injustice we do to children is our contemporary idealization of them. In the modern book if a child misbehaves or is "socially maladjusted," it is all the fault of its parents or other adults. The child in this picture comes into the world pure as snow and the characteristics it subsequently develops merely reflect its environment. There is never the necessity to reform the child. What is needed is the reform of its parents, preferably with the aid of a professional psychiatrist. Parents must subject themselves, render themselves all but incapable of thought, turn their homes (adults live in homes, too) upside down in order to avoid cultivating "tensions" in their young ones.

All this leaves out of account the fact that healthy children are, among other things, little animals, who only slowly evolve (if they ever do) into civilized human beings, and that the process of so evolving is painful to them, and to their caretakers as well, and under even the best conditions. Children are not naturally "good," according to any standards ever set by a civilized society. They are natural barbarians. They are largely instinctual, acquisitive, aggressive, inquisitive, affectionate, imitative, playful, braggadocious, and cruel. Children — perfectly "normal" children — are at some stage of their development given to thievery, vandalism, exhibitionism, deception, simulation, and exploitation.

They are not naturally modest nor naturally clean. A cat toilet-trains her kitten almost as soon as it is born, but it is a struggle to toilet-train a human infant. The psychiatrists are now keeping mothers changing and washing diapers much longer than any mothers did before, lest baby become neurotic as the result of Mama's "compulsively neat basic neurosis." For generations mothers have been taking baby from his "nice warm cot and putting him on a cold, cold pot, whether he wanted to or not," and early or late, baby has never liked it. The psychiatrists themselves were early toilet-trained; everyone their age was. That the process of diapering baby long after he can walk might conceivably create a neurosis in Mama doesn't matter.

Children are little anarchists, possessed, however, of a powerful herd instinct, leading them to demand oppressive conformity from others, and especially conformity to their own primitive urges. The parental and educational function, however, is so to train, influence, and govern these little barbarians that a civilized adult can endure living with them, and that they may also, in time, become civilized adults themselves. Otherwise human society would consist only of grown-up children with adult powers at the service of their primitive instincts, than which no prospect is more appalling.

But the exercise of the educational function *always*, and *in nature*, encounters rebellion. The best book Professor Freud ever wrote is in my opinion his short little essay, "Civilization and its Discontents." Civilization, as he points out, is *not* natural. It involves constant and painful repressions of primitive natural urges, which continually lurk beneath the surface ready to break through every fissure in the social fabric. Civilization, in short, has to pay off or natural man will destroy it.

The child is "natural man," with all the charm of natural man — his exuberance, imagination, curiosity, insouciance, affection, but *also* his brutishness. Civilization is cultivation and domestication. It involves the taming of some natural instincts and the cultivation of others.

But however one looks at it, it involves taming. And taming, however gently accomplished, requires authority. No one can tame an animal who is afraid of the animal, and no one can tame a child who is afraid of the child. If he is, the child will "drive him wild," and, naturally, his wildness will drive the child wilder.

Lest someone at this point express shocked horror at my reporting on the little ones, let me make a confession. What I know about children is mostly derived from what I remember from having once been a child.

From vivid memory I can assert that if my parents and teachers had not succeeded in blocking many of my natural tendencies, and by a combination of force, reward, and the invocation of authority, human and divine, I would have been a private and public scourge. Yet I was certainly "normal" — no better or worse than my brother, sister, and most of my school and play mates. I was formidably healthy, bursting with energy, and reasonably bright. Despite the fact that my young, loving, and greatly lovable mother died when I was seven, I had a happy and affectionate childhood home. Mother was succeeded by my father's sister, Aunt Elizabeth, twenty years his senior, a mother and grandmother. She was a genius with children. I think she may have learned much from bringing up her own. When she came to us, her genius consisted in really liking us, while "taking no nonsense" from us whatsoever. We knew exactly where we stood with Aunt Lizzie, as we had earlier known where we stood with our more imaginative mother.

In Aunt Lizzie's cosmos, home and school were benevolent despotisms where children behaved themselves. In a village pastor's household there were no servants. Aunt Lizzie, a stickler for order and cleanliness, had not the slightest intention of "wearing herself to the bone," picking and cleaning up after disorderly children. When we were big enough to reach them, we each had to make our own beds — and make them exactly as they should be made. If we rushed with muddy feet upon an immaculate floor, Aunt Lizzie would direct our attention to the mop, and sit placidly in a rocking chair while we cleaned up the mess we had made. When we played with our toys on the sitting room floor, we had to put them away afterward, in the cupboard where they belonged.

We could be as noisy as we liked if Father was not in his study. Otherwise she would shoo us into the yard. Aunt Lizzie held the opinion highly heretical today that the comfort and convenience of adults should be considered, that there was no happy home without happy parents, and that civilized adults could not live happily in bedlam.

No child ever said "I won't" to Aunt Lizzie — or said it more than once or twice. Aunt Lizzie's response was grim and automatic — a stinging hand applied to the spot designed for that purpose. Aunt Lizzie never nagged. She acted. She never argued. She judged.

Why did we so love her (though we sometimes shook impotent fists behind her back) that when we get together today, parents and grandparents ourselves, we always speak of her and the thought of her always makes us grin?

For one thing "she saw right through us." It was perfectly futile to lie to Aunt Lizzie. "Now that you've finished that cock-and-bull story," Aunt Lizzie would say (she was rather given to clichés), "what really happened?" Aunt Lizzie, though, didn't seem to think the cock-and-bull story a terrible crime. She *expected* it. She knew we were natural liars. She *understood* us. That was a comfort. Aunt Lizzie never believed you to be better than you were! And anticipating the worst, she was sometimes agreeably surprised!

Aunt Lizzie, also, was as prompt with rewards as with punishments. When I got a report card with four A's we had ice cream and angel food cake for supper, in my honor, and she didn't chide me for being rather smug about the achievement. How strange is memory, that I can recall every detail of that festivity so many many years ago!

Aunt Lizzie was a most comforting lap and bosom on which to cry out one's real griefs — like the quarrel with Marguerite, which seemed, then, to interrupt forever my greatest friendship — but she quickly detected phony ones. When I came sniveling home from school, complaining that Miss Bliss had rapped my hand with a ruler, and that it "hurt terribly," Aunt Lizzie, who knew Miss Bliss, didn't even examine the hand. She only remarked, "I'm sure you richly deserved it." I *did* deserve it, and I knew it. I had put the whole class in an uproar with the device of a spool of thread in a tin can, secreted in the desk of one of my class "enemies," with the thread in my own hand, to make a clatter during recitations, and direct the blame upon my pet hate — at the time.

Today's Aunt Lizzie would probably call a mass meeting of parents to protest Miss Bliss's cruelty. It is unfashionable to speak of the cruelty of children to teachers.

Life in home and school was routine. Family prayers at 7.30, breakfast at 8, school from 9 to 12 and 1 to 3. Homework from 5 to 6.

Homework! Aunt Lizzie was the disciplinarian but Father the educator and inspirer. In the hierarchy of authority, God came first, but was very far away, Father next, also a little far away, and Aunt Lizzie right down to earth and on hand. Father always had time to supervise homework — never to do it for us, but to see that we did it; to be on hand to answer questions. Apropos of a theme: "There are three misspelled words."

"How do you spell them, Papa?"

"Look them up in the dictionary, dear."

Home parties. Rainy afternoons with all our friends in the kitchen, making fudge, pulling taffy, in a fair amount of uproar. But everything was conditional. We couldn't leave the candy pots for Aunt Lizzie to wash.

Where, in this ordered and benevolently controlled life, did we work off our "tensions" and "unblock our aggressions"?

We worked them off in the streets, woods, fields, back lots, woodsheds and barns of the small towns where we lived. Supervised *play* was confined to a neighbor's occasional glance from a sitting room window. We expressed part of our rebellion against law by defying the laws of nature — jumping out of tall haylofts with an umbrella for a parachute, trying to walk the tight rope of a knife-edged roof-tree, skating on thin ice and falling through, riding farm horses bareback and being thrown, negotiating icy hills with bobsleds and running into wagon teams. Casualties were numerous — broken bones, sprains, abrasions. I can hardly remember myself between the ages of nine and twelve without a bandage or a scab.

Out of doors and among ourselves we led our natural life, surcharged, quarrelsome, wild, imaginative, and secret — from adults. The hut we built in the woods, the cave-rooms excavated in snow, the secrets we told each other, the raids we made on orchards and melon patches, the incantations we chanted like witches in the church cemetery firmly believing they would cause the demise of some particular adult against whom we had sworn vengeance. Yet, with it all, the sense of wonder, sometimes amounting to ecstasy, at the mysterious beauty of the world around us — conscious in fleeting moments of the loveliness of skunk cabbage in April, the miracle of the showy lady's-slipper in June, the splendor of the autumnal maple tree. After all the wildness, bringing a bouquet of field flowers home to arrange in a vase, for father's study.

In the wild, barbarian vacation hours of our lives, we did many things of which our parents would not approve, and learned many things in a very rude, coarse way. It was a curiously dual life: the kind but firm severity of home and school; the unbridled private and herd life outside their walls — a combination of healthful care and healthy neglect.

But they complemented each other.

When we came home, exhausted, to have our wounds bound up (matter-of-factly, "If you *will* do such things, you must take the consequences," and ouch, the iodine!) home was shelter and haven. Then we were grateful — grateful for hot gingerbread; for the twinkle of a cozy fire; for father's kind steady face, and the noble stories he read us, creating our heroes; for Aunt Lizzie's calm voice of authority; for the cool, clean bed; for peace and security. Grateful, in short, for order and civilization, which tangibly paid off.

And so before we rush to psychiatrists about Bob's or Mary's or our own "complexes," let us know, let us love, let us remember — what we once were ourselves.

The Moments That Educate

In all that is said and written about "education," moral, intellectual, and utilitarian, to which in these pages I have from time to time contributed my own ideas, we usually, I think, overlook a main point.

As I look back upon my life, trying to analyze the educational factors that have most contributed to making me what I am, for better or worse, I realize that what I was formally taught in school or college has had a relatively small effect. What, from school, became part of me, was not what I "learned," but the windows that were opened in my mind in the process of learning. Although, for instance, I was a good Latin student in high school and college, I would be hard put to it today to make a sight translation of any Latin prose or poetry not already familiar from translation. But I owe an unending interest in the antique world, its world outlook, philosophy, art, and values to the windows opened in my mind by a Latin teacher in Lewis Institute, Chicago, where I had my high school training — the late George B. Tenney.

The examples could be multiplied by scores. Many seeds fall into the mind of a child or adolescent, some to take root and others to perish, and it is hard to say just why. In every young person's life, also, there are crises — moral or intellectual — and how they are responded to often depends upon the guidance on hand at the given moment.

I know, for instance, exactly when and where I first became aware of the existence of social classes, an awareness initially accompanied by shock, envy, grief, shame, and resentment. Had these reactions, however repressed, continued to fester, they would, I am inclined to think, have influenced my life and attitudes and not for my future contentment or happiness. But an immediate intervention prevented that. The instrument was my father.

When I was a little over ten, the "Conference" to which my Methodist minister father belonged — "the faith," as he used to quip, "which moves parsons" — transferred him to a new parish, or "charge."

Hitherto, from the time I had begun to notice things at all, our successive parsonage homes had been in villages of two to four thousand people, all of them serving surrounding agricultural communities. Each contained families who were well or less well off, a status reflected in whether they lived in larger or smaller houses, with wider or narrower yards, or whether (which in those days was rare) they owned an automobile.

But the differences were in degree, not in kind. The presidents of the creamery and the local bank, the owner of the biggest hardware, "drygoods," or grocery stores, the man who did the largest insurance business, and often the most popular doctor lived in the larger houses, their children had more nickels to spend on licorice whips, horehound drops, and milk chocolate, and had shinier bicycles, and their small daughters (I don't remember about the sons) had several "best dresses" instead of one. But we all wore the same kind of clothes, every kid's spending money was in nickels — I never saw one flash a dollar bill — and our mothers did all of their housework, or were aided by a "hired girl," a farmer's daughter who lived as part of the family, or by neighbors who came to "help out" for an hourly fee, none of them regarded by themselves or their employers as servants, and often, like the older persons working in the stores, calling their employers by their first names.

In these villages my father, as an educated man and a clergyman, was definitely among the "leading citizens," and although we lived austerely, not to say penuriously, I never had any feeling of inferiority.

My father's new parish was different. Its backbone occupations were still services to the surrounding farmers, but it was a larger town, with several prosperous mills. These were largely family concerns with financial cross-pollination. They also did their banking locally, and the bank president was one of them. So a few families were rich, not just "well off." They lived in homes surrounded not by "yards," however pretty, but by expansive, beautifully kept gardens.

Still, the new two-story parsonage was the finest and most commodious house we had ever occupied, with a parlor, sitting room, dining room, study, and large, if old-fashioned kitchen on the first floor and four bedrooms, a bathroom, and a small unfinished attic on the second. For the first time I lived in a house with a full bathroom, and had a room of my own!

If its furniture, collected by the parsonage committee, was heterogeneous and ill-matched — Victorian sofas upholstered in horsehair, a "patent" rocking chair covered with worn Brussels carpeting, a remarkable combination writing desk, bookcase, and chest of drawers of "golden oak" with an oval mirror set in one side of the upper cabinet, giving the piece the look of a one-eyed monster — it was the kind of furniture to which I was accustomed, and not only in parsonages furnished by lady committees. Altogether, it seemed to my childish eyes palatial!

Of course I had no knowledge of the economic structure of the town, nor was yet aware that the local rich never sent their offspring to the town's high school, but East, to private boarding schools, and thence to Harvard, Yale, or Dartmouth. None of them was a member of my father's church; they were Episcopalians or Presbyterians, and their ministers did not wear Prince Alberts on weekdays, as did my father, for he had no other, but business suits, or tweed jackets — all of which I was only later to observe.

But the "hill set" did send their children to grade school, where I promptly made a friend, who asked me to "luncheon" the following Saturday.

Her home, set in a professionally landscaped garden, was impressive from the outside, and when I rang the bell the door was opened by a gentleman in a striped waistcoat and a funny little jacket, who announced that "Miss" Fanny was expect-

ing me and would I please go upstairs — up a very wide
winding staircase with a delicate rail, the like of which I had
never seen, sweeping up from an enormous lounge-hall in
which I stood completely overcome. The floor was so polished that I glanced for my own reflection as in a pool, and
on it lay silky rugs of jewel colors, like islands of enamel.
Deep-cushioned chairs were covered with ruby damask-silk,
of which the draperies at the long windows were also made,
and along the pale high walls were delicate chairs with fretted
backs and small pedestaled tables, on which were enormous
bowls of autumn roses and chrysanthemums. At the right,
through a wide-open door, I saw the gleaming dark wood of
a dining table, set with no tablecloth but lacy mats and
twinkling silver, and at the left, through a similar doorway, a
room even larger than the one where I stood, with walls of
palest green, silken curtains of darker jade, a rug all rubies,
emeralds, topazes, turquoises covering the whole floor, more
chairs surely not designed to be sat on, flowers again, and
everywhere the most wonderful smell, of roses, lavender, I
knew not what.

A devouring bookworm, I had read of castles and palaces,
but they were just in books, in stories, made up, not real.

A voice from the stairtop called "Miss" Dorothy, in an odd
accent, and slowly I mounted the stairs, which again opened
into a wide hall with many doors. One was open to a room
in which sat my classmate, before a mirrored table. She wore
a slip with a round neck, white and fine as silk, edged top and
bottom with delicate lace, and a lady in a beautiful black silk
dress, frilly apron, and tiny lace cap was brushing her long
hair. "Good morning, miss," she said to me, and Fanny, leap-
ing up said, "Goody! You've come! This is Marie. She's
Ma's maid but she takes care of me, too."

What a strange house where grownups called children
"Miss" and children called grownups by their first names!

And Fanny's room! Why it was bigger than our parlor and sitting room together, with pale gold-colored furniture all matching, a long bookcase, the color of the pale blue walls, frilly curtains, and draperies and chairs sprinkled all over with roses.

I stood in a "Peter Thompson" sailor suit, conscious for the first time in my life that its blue serge cloth was coarse, that the let-down skirt had a faint line from the earlier hem, that my shoes, though vigorously polished, were scuffed.

Fanny chattered gaily, her dressing being completed, while I, with my heart burning in me like a fire, surveyed the books, remarking superiorly that I had read them all, didn't she think they were "childish"? — I was reading *The Outcasts* by Victor Hugo, who was French. Marie having left the room, Fanny explained that she was French, Ma had brought her from Paris and Ma spoke French, too. I announced my pahpie spoke Latin — a gross exaggeration, but greatly impressive to Fanny — and that I contemplated learning all the languages in the world, including Chinee, to which the wide-eyed Fanny asked "Whyever *for?*" regretting, "I'll *have* to learn French but I don't want to."

I flaunted my intellectual interests (hitherto nonexistent or unconscious), with Fanny listening admiringly all through lunch, which was dinner to me, with clear soup in cups, and fresh meat (our Sunday treat) and ice cream, all served from silver dishes on gold-edged plates by the gentleman in the striped vest. We were alone — Ma, Fanny explained, having gone riding. I made another mental memo that Fanny's mother had nothing more to do than ride a horse, while my auntie at that moment was doubtless baking bread.

I broke away then, as quickly as I could, and when I was beyond the grounds, burst into bitter tears. It was so *beautiful* — a house one lived in could be *beautiful* — and I hated it, hated Fanny, hated myself. I was ashamed, and worst of all, a feeling accompanied by a crushing sense of guilt, I was ashamed of my father! Like being ashamed of God! I did not see him as a face but as a suit of clothes walking, clothes no one else wore, shiny and greenish at the elbows.

As I approached the parsonage I saw for the first time its skimpy windows, which seemed to be making mean faces at me. Its narrow hall closed like prison walls, and looking into the sitting room I saw the threadbare patch before the sofa, discouraging as a sigh.

I crept up to my bedroom, whose privacy only that morning had delighted me. Now it appeared as a narrow box papered hideously, its iron brass-trimmed bed, with a plain white spread, the chest of drawers, from which a shred of paint hung like loose skin, and one straight "golden oak" chair filling it but for a narrow passage between bed and wall and bed and chest, on which lay two small rag mats. I guessed that even the servants in the big house had better rooms. And lying on the bed, under the spread, I cried silently, hopelessly, in furious revolt against all this ugliness.

My aunt, looking for me at suppertime, thought I slept, though I was feigning it, not wanting among other things to see her apron, and reported to my father her anxiety that I must be sick because I'd never gone to bed in my life without being urged.

But my father, who knew me best, came up after supper, turned on the gas light, sat on the edge of the bed, felt my pulse, saw it was normal, and regarded my smeared cheeks and red eyes. He went right to the heart of the matter. "You were at Fanny's today, and saw a beautiful home, and are envious and discontented." It was not an accusation. I turned my eyes from him for the treason in my heart, but nodded.

"Get up," he said, "and come downstairs. You should eat some supper." I murmured that I was not hungry — though

I had only picked at the fine luncheon — but I got up, being unaccustomed to disobey, and we went downstairs together, through the kitchen, where Auntie, buttering bread, said nothing, and into the garden. Night falls early and swiftly in the autumn, the stars were out and a sickle moon, and trees and shrubbery only faint dark masses. We sat on a wooden bench.

"Do you wish on the first star you see?" asked my father's voice lightly. "Then wish to learn how to be happy."

"Star-light, star-bright, first star I've seen tonight," I murmured obediently, not making any wish aloud.

"Where Fanny lives is so lovely — like in a story — and it gives me a pain here," I opened up with my hand on my heart.

"Is it more lovely than the stars?" I heard a voice with humor in it.

"Different from the stars," I said.

"If we sit here more and more will come out. You know how they make pictures in the sky, each in its own constellation: Andromeda, Cassiopeia, Lyra, the Bear. (Lovely words: Andromeda, Cassiopeia.) The astronomers say each great star is a world, each has its place in the scheme of the universe. Look how they differ from each other. Follow along from the handle of the Dipper — that big, blue, sparkling star is Arcturus. They say it is the star that guided the wise men to Bethlehem. But Sirius is brightest. And Antares is red. See?

"The universe is greater than the greatest mind can comprehend," the voice from the dimness went on. "Even our whole wide world within it is but a tiny part. And in that small world the largest, grandest house ever built is — like an almost invisible speck."

"Yes, but some people *do* have big beautiful houses and some littler and ugly ones."

"Everybody born has something more and something less than others. Some have food but no appetite. Some own beauty but have no eyes to see. Some see beauty all around them without wanting to own it. Some have clever hands and some clever heads."

"Who are the richest?"

"Those who have love" — the words came lightly.

After a pause he asked, "What is the nicest taste?"

"Ice cream," I replied promptly.

"Are you sure? Is it better than the taste of an apple? How does an apple taste?"

This was a game we often played at home, describing the tastes, sounds, smells, and touch of things.

"It tastes like autumn," I said, "like frost and red leaves. It is cool and wet and crunchy, like when you walk in snow. You taste it in your teeth, too."

"Is ice cream better than the taste of bread?"

"With butter on it?"

"Bread and butter," my father agreed.

"Bread tastes brown and white and hard and soft," I attempted. "It tastes chewy, like butternuts, and smooth like cream. Like cream and nuts."

"If you were very, very hungry?"

"Like when your stomach feels squeaky?"

"Yes, like that. Then what would taste better, bread or ice cream?"

Ice cream, I thought, would taste cold — all the way down into the rattle. "I think for a shivery stomach bread would be more — cozy."

"I think so too," my father laughed. "Definitely more cozy.

"So, you see, between big and little, great and small, rich and poor, bread and butter and ice cream, there is proportion. To see things in proportion helps us to be happy. Those who have milk and bread and butter, a snug shelter, a bed for sleep, a fire when it is cold, a breeze when it is warm, have all they really need of such things. And if not everyone has even these, it means people are not helping God answer the prayer they pray. God intends everyone to have his daily bread, and earn it for himself, unless of course he is sick or old, and then his neighbors must furnish it, with love. But if that sort of thing were all we had, we would be poor indeed."

"What else do we have, anyhow?"

"Beauty, my child, beauty!" Now the voice was impatient. "Beauty everywhere — in the sky, in people's faces, in books, in pictures, in poems, in a tree. Have you read *Walden* yet?"

"No, but I will, Pahpie."

He changed the subject. "I hope you and Fanny will be friends," he said. "People say she is lonely. She is an only child, you know, and her mother is busy with other things."

"She rides a horse," I confided. "Every single day. She wasn't home for lunch."

"She travels a great deal," said my father, "and leaves Fanny to the servants."

"The man at lunch didn't even talk," I said. "Just passed things."

"And I suspect some of the other village children feel the way you once did," said my father blandly, referring to the distant past of a previous hour.

Pity for Fanny overwhelmed my highly susceptible nature. No brother to romp with, no little sister to pet or scold, no games at the table, no Auntie!

"Is envy a very bad sin?" I inquired. "Do I get punished?"

"Envy is its own punishment," replied my father. "But I will sentence you to learn a Psalm:

'The heavens declare the glory of God, and the firmament showeth his handiwork.'"

Readers will protest that I cannot possibly recall such a conversation verbatim after many years. Of course they are right. What I recall are all my feelings, my father's reaction to them, and the gist of our conversation. I have recalled them again, and again, throughout my life, in similar circumstances of frustrated desires and ambitions. That is what I mean by the moments that open windows which never again are wholly closed.

We went into the house, finally, for it had grown chilly outside. Auntie had laid a clean napkin on the corner of the kitchen table. The gas cast a yellow gleam and the wood range filled the room with warmth. The other children must have gone to bed. At the place laid for me there were soft-boiled eggs in a cup, a glass of milk, fresh homemade buttered bread, a dish of apple sauce. I was ravenous.

"It tastes good, Auntie," I said shyly. "I like it here."

"To be sure it does," she said. "To be sure you do."

The Baby in the Kitchen

TWENTY-FOUR years ago in early July a two-week-old baby came to Twin Farms, our home in Vermont. He was my baby. Everything had been prepared for his arrival: a sunny nursery, immaculately and sanitarily white with an adjoining room and bath for the trained baby-nurse I had employed, both as far removed as possible from the study of his father, a famous writer, and from the normal traffic of the house.

Twenty-four years ago the services of an experienced baby-nurse, cook, housemaid, and gardener could be obtained for less than a not-at-all-experienced couple would cost today, and the baby's father was well able to afford such a staff, and two secretaries, and occasional hourly help for the garden as well.

In such a household there was complete division of labor. The cook cooked and took care of the kitchen; the housemaid cared for the other rooms; the gardener had a room outside the house and appeared only briefly for meals; the secretaries lived outside and came from nine to one and two to five; and nurse, who had her meals on a tray, took entire care of the baby and the nursery, and had no other duties.

During the weeks when I was able to nurse him, I appeared at 10, 2, and 6 P.M. in the nursery to perform that function, and for night feedings nurse brought him to my bedside. If he cried at other times (or yelled — a baby's cries are tearless) nobody heard him but nurse. She changed and washed his diapers and clothes, and brought him in daily for the brief admiration of his parents, exquisitely dressed, pleasantly redolent of violet-scented talcum, and either peacefully asleep or contentedly and equally peacefully awake.

Apart from the attentions of the white-uniformed, quiet, and perfectly efficient nurse he lived in almost complete isolation, a cocoon-like existence. Babies, I had been advised, should not be fondled. They should not be subject to noises. They should be kept aloof from company who might carry germs. They must always be bathed and fed at exactly the same time and preferably by the same person. They should never be rocked. They should never be given *any* medicine except on the advice of a pediatrician. They should be kept away from bright lights. And since he was my first baby, born late in my life and likely to be my only one, I did exactly what the doctor told me for the apple of my eye.

He was a healthy baby. He cost me no sleepless nights and no cares. The only "sacrifices" I endured were not being able to go to a party or visit a neighbor or be with friends in my own house while I was nursing him, at nursing hours.

To be sure, I used to wonder how babies survived who couldn't be brought up in nurseries by trained attendants, or by mothers with nothing else to do; how, in fact, I and my brother and sister had survived in blooming health reared as we were in a far more haphazard fashion. Later, I observed that my little boy, no longer a baby, was more nervous than most, and more easily upset by strange faces or noises, and that the infant who led a germless existence caught as a child every ailment — scarlet fever, measles, chicken pox, mumps, whooping cough — that cropped up in a radius of twenty-five miles. But I never really questioned whether the whole pattern of his baby care might not have been ideal.

This summer another two-week-old baby came with his mother to Twin Farms — the son of that first baby. His father was employed in a summer theater and their New York apartment was sublet, so Baby's first home, like his father's, was the Vermont house — capacious, its gardens wide, but the household arrangements very different from what they were twenty-four years ago.

The house, staffed by a neighbor and her daughter, both mothers and one a grandmother, plus my secretary, is not run on a defined system of division of labor, but the way those houses of families who do their own work are run: one doing most but not all of the cooking, another most but not always all of the housework, and everybody pitching in within the limits of her free time to lend a hand. In this house the kitchen, once the rather remote domain of a professional cook, is the hub of the home. Here, in addition to daily meals being prepared, vegetables are canned or sterilized for the freezer, chickens are drawn, butter is churned, even lambs or a veal are cut up and wrapped for the freezer, the latter invariably done by my artist husband, who finds the study of anatomy good training for a butcher.

Redesigned three years ago by *The Ladies' Home Journal* to fit just such a home-economy as ours, it is, with a room-size pantry and "summer kitchen" flanking it, a big, very beautiful kitchen, with every modern convenience, including electric range and ovens. But the old wood range is still there. This past summer in northern New England was uniquely chilly and rainy, a furnace fire was too hot, and in the living rooms fireplaces took off the chill. But the cheery wood range warmed the kitchen and back of the house, exuding a pleasant aromatic smell. And as everyone, at some time during the day, gravitates toward the kitchen, so did Baby, his pretty bassinet on wheels landing plump in the middle of everything, in front of the kitchen stove, with an opened oven door, or, when it was warm and sunny, on the veranda right outside the south kitchen windows.

A young mother needs rests, especially when she must soon face caring for Baby alone and doing her housework too. Her nights were interrupted by feeding her son, nestled in the basket beside her bed. So who took care of Baby during the day while his mother was resting? Everybody did — whoever was nearest — and with Baby in the kitchen someone was always at hand to lay aside a duster or turn from a pot or run in from an adjoining room in response to his cries.

Was he rocked? He certainly was — a foot pushing his bassinet back and forth while its owner's hands peeled potatoes or shelled peas.

Was he always fed at exactly the prescribed hour? He was not. "He's sleeping so sweetly I wouldn't wake him up," one of baby's numerous attendants would say. Or, "That cry means hunger, and it's clear he just didn't get enough to eat last time. Why not give him a little supplementary bottle?

I've brought up too many babies to think there can be fixed rules."

Was he picked up? He certainly was, and carried and crooned to, and by everybody. Our neighbor, the writer Vincent Sheean, who often dropped in, proved an especially acceptable baby-walker. He explained learnedly that his forearm was exactly the right length, to the fraction of an inch, to permit him to cradle Baby's head in his elbow and hold his bottom in his hand; that Baby's obvious preference for him was purely due to this mechanical fact — this to spare the feelings of the rest of us. Just the same, it was obvious that he considered the pacifying effect of his presence a feather in his cap, a refutation of his reputation for artistic erraticism, and a demonstration that he was altogether a superior fellow (as indeed he is) and one in whom a helpless infant could properly repose complete confidence.

When, though warm, dry, and fed, Baby cried, cramping up his legs in an obvious touch of the colic, it was the consensus of the four mothers that two drops of peppermint oil in some warm water "certainly could do him no harm" — and he quieted down.

Most of the time he slept, while the traffic milled around him, in the midst of conversation, kitchen noises, kitchen lights, and kitchen smells, or gazed up calmly at the many faces of the household, of visitors, of house guests, of children who stopped at his cradle to cluck admiringly. Of course he interrupted the housework. But "Don't bother about my room — I'll make my own bed," said a house guest. "Let *me* dust the big living room," said another, their services gratefully accepted.

After dinner my helpmates go to their own homes and families. Then Baby was wherever the family and visitors foregathered. I would never have dreamed of nursing my child in company, but this baby's young mother saw no reason why she should leave a pleasant tea party of intimate friends, or withdraw from a conversation, to feed her tiny son. When we were invited out to dinner we went — and took the baby, who seemed to love the motion of a car and to slumber as well in one place as in another.

To be sure, having the baby in the midst of everything was sometimes a nuisance and occasionally aroused protests. Even I put my foot down when, on a rainy day, I found a rack of baby clothes drying over the register in the dining room, where we were about to have lunch, and my husband declared, "This house is becoming a slum."

A friend had sent Baby, as a christening present, a funny little doll to tie to his bassinet, which, wound up, played the famous Brahms cradle song. Baby liked it. If he was restless the sound composed him, and it tinkled from the kitchen, the living room, the veranda, or wherever Baby happened to be. It is a charming tune — or I used to think so. Eventually the sound became a mild torture, not the less so because everyone went around humming it. "Couldn't we find *another* music box — one that would play the *Mozart* cradle song for a change?" I found myself complaining.

This, however, I observed. Babies (as do cows and chickens) like music. Or at least this one did. He went happily to sleep in the living room to the thunder of Shostakovitch's *Fifth Symphony*, or the death aria from *Boris Godounov*, or Gershwin's *Rhapsody in Blue*, played on the phonograph.

Heated discussions over EDC and "reappraisals of foreign policy" had an equally soporific effect. He appeared to retire from the conversation in sheer boredom — a depressing suggestion that Grandma's holding forth might have the same effect on grownups if they had not learned to be polite.

The point is that against all the advocates of "peace and quiet" in Baby's surroundings, this one undoubtedly preferred goings-on. His big, beautiful violet-blue eyes — "all babies of the Caucasian race are born with blue eyes and his may turn out to be brown or hazel or any old color," the Harvard professor from next door warned us — would turn toward the sound of a voice, or a tune, or a movement, though he could not yet see more than light and shadow. The sense of life around him seemed to give him unconscious comfort. And why shouldn't it? Especially since the two mothers, two grandmothers, stepgrandfather, baby-crazy secretary, neighbors' children, Harvard professor, visiting guests, and Mr. Sheean were approving and solicitous. Is affection not a form of radiant warmth?

The stepgrandfather had determined not to be taken in. "I want to make it clear I will *not* be disturbed by the baby," he had said. How surprising, then, to find the baby on his arm, looking up at him with a wide appraising gaze. "He was yelling like an angry Slovak," he explained defensively. "With all you women around — what a house! — can't *somebody* attend to this child?"

I explained weakly that babies can't be waited on hand and foot every time they cry. "He'll grow into a little tyrant."

"Nonsense," said the big man whose crossness is always phony.

After five weeks, Baby and his mother had to leave, to rejoin his father in New York. The station wagon drew up at the summer-kitchen door, packed with bathinette, bassinet, chest of drawers, scales, clothes rack — what a moving! Baby in his mother's arms (he had just been fed) gazed brightly and I thought quite callously on us all.

Never kiss a baby? Everybody kissed him, in turn — on the top of his head. Grandmother Alice's eyes filled with tears; Mother Irene burst into sobs; Grandma Dorothy assumed a matter-of-fact stoicism. Secretary Ginny (who was driving them down) looked coolly efficient, but still a little nervous over her responsibility.

"Well," said stepgrandfather, "the mess is over. What a *happy* mess!"

"Now I must really concentrate on my work," I said — knowing that what I'd concentrate on was missing the baby.

In the kitchen the oven door of the wood range was closed. There was no rack of drying baby clothes, no bassinet, no tinkle of the Brahms cradle song.

"This kitchen seems absolutely empty," said Alice, wiping her eyes.

There were four of us in it at the time.

Why and What Should Johnny Read?

FEW ARTICLES that have appeared in this space have awakened so large a response as the one in the July issue entitled "Why Make It Harder for Johnny to Read?"

That article, largely confined to *methods* of teaching reading, with emphasis upon the departure from the phonic processes in use for thousands of years in all languages that have an alphabet, with the consequent limitation on vocabulary, aroused a considerable controversy, though it received a confirmative response of more than five to one. Readers who wrote to express either agreement or dissent included parents and teachers, and their letters revealed them to be, with few exceptions, people who had given much thought to the problems involved in the evolution of primary education in reading.

Many, especially the teachers who wrote, threw new light on the question out of their own experiences, and the file of their responses constitutes a valuable social and educational document in itself.

A recurrent request was "Please write more on this subject."

Meanwhile, my own interest in preparing the July article had been aroused to investigate and think further on the subject of the American child's primary accomplishment, basic to all education, the capacity to learn from written words.

The problem involves many questions besides the one of how Johnny can best learn to read writings. What is the *purpose* in teaching a child to read? Is it only to develop what the professional educators now call a "functional skill," and which *seems* to mean a skill necessary to a person's functioning as an employable person or a literate citizen, or one able to continue his education for the sake of the more efficient performing of "function"? If this be so, it is possible that in the universal push to abolish illiteracy we may create the phenomenon of literates illiterate in every higher sense. Perhaps the educators will enlighten me on the meaning of the adjective "functional" modifying "skill," for such works of theirs as I have read have not made it clear to me.

At any rate, our forefathers, engaged in educating the young, wrote and talked in a language understandable to all, and not in the bureaucratic "expertise" that increasingly walls off the educational profession from everybody except the graduates of teachers' colleges. Earlier educators make their purposes clear in the yellowing pages of old textbooks, the "readers" that it is hard to find today except in well-stocked public or university libraries, from which they are seldom withdrawn.

As I write I am flanked on one side by such old books, made available to me by courtesy of the splendid library of Dartmouth College. And on the other side are piled Readers in use in our schools today.

The old "Readers" were numerous. Different ones were used in various regions of our country. Because of the restrictions of space, I am confining myself, for purposes of illustration in discussing the old ones, to the McGuffey Readers from the second grade onward as used in most of the schools of the Middle West and South during the later nineteenth century until the dawn of "modern" education.

William McGuffey, president of two Ohio colleges and ultimately Professor of Moral Philosophy at the University of Virginia, never heard the phrase "functional skill," but he had a clear conception, shared by the editors of other contemporary Readers here and abroad, of what children should learn by reading.

It went far beyond training the child to distinguish words "in meaningful context," necessary, of course, to reading anything from a business letter to verbalized trash.

The McGuffey Readers, from the time that children knew their letters and could visually recognize a few hundred simple words they had long known by ear, purposefully concentrated on introducing children to the finest literature in existence, at levels they could understand; in communicating to them, via such literature, the highest thoughts, ethical principles, and moral precepts; of using such literature to familiarize them with history, geography, philosophical concepts, the wonders of nature and of human experience, and the lives of great men. Children were exercised in reading such literature aloud, with proper diction and with such emphasis on the right words that the meaning of every passage and the child's comprehension of it were revealed by the *way* in which he read it.

Now, fine literature, even such as is consciously written for children, cannot be created out of a meager vocabulary, much of it proper names (Mary, Jack) or names of common objects (chair, train, dish), especially if the author has to produce lessons in which each new word must be repeated ten times, and words learned in a previous lesson five times. A new reading series (in the teachers' edition that the children do not know) boasts that this has been done. But discriminating writers are usually quite unable to play this sort of game, so the modern Readers are not written by writers, but by tailors of words to suit the methodology and keep the reading matter within the range of the average child's vocabulary as determined by "experts" — expert, be it said, on the basis of tests of their own methods.

The old Readers assumed that a child could comprehend at a quite early age a very large number of words, if they appeared in a mentally and imaginatively stimulating context. Neither editors nor teachers wrote texts above the second or third grades or employed anyone else to write them. The Readers are "eclectic," and so described. They are selections from literature, great either by the test of having survived decades, scores, or hundreds of years, or by the higher critical standards of the day. A school child, brought up on the McGuffey Readers, was expected by the end of the second grade to command a reading (and spelling) vocabulary of at least 2000 words, while a child taught by the reading methods and matter of a modern series in wide use is confined to a vocabulary of 875.

Inspection reveals that the form and content of the old Readers was far better by literary standards than those of today, and the rate of reading progress much faster. A fourth-grade child, at the average age of ten, was reading in simplified form in the McGuffey Readers some of the great stories of the Bible, closely resembling the original text, and in the fifth grade unmodified excerpts from the King James Version and from the original and unsimplified writings of Washington Irving, Hawthorne, Samuel Johnson, Daniel Webster, Rousseau, Jefferson, and Oliver Goldsmith; poems by Bryant, Whittier, and Byron; passages from Shakespeare, and from other writers esteemed throughout Western civilization at the time.

A twelve-year-old, in the sixth McGuffey Reader, had a fare which, and I say it advisedly, would be beyond the vocabulary or comprehension of some American college students today. It not only included passages from Dickens, Scott, Irving, Bulwer-Lytton, and Schiller, but from the speeches and writings of statesmen — Disraeli, Fox, Pitt, Walpole, Patrick Henry, Webster, Addison, Blackstone, Chatham — and the great English and American poets. The twelve-year-old American child was introduced, via Pope's translation, to Homer; to the great German poet Herder; to Milton, Southey, Leigh Hunt, and Poe, along with more Shakespeare, the Bible, and popular and narrative poets. The works he read contained many internal literary or historical allusions that had, at the outset, to be explained — references to Socrates, Plato, and other Greek philosophers. As for vocabulary, any twelve-year-old who could read with comprehension McGuffey's Sixth Reader, could read, I should think anything in the English language, and since he was tested by having to answer questions regarding content, and make précis, he had to know the meaning of what he had read.

In contrast, the Fourth Readers in the modern series I am also reviewing (and it is one of the best) contains only five works by authors of established literary reputation: Chaucer, Dorothy Canfield Fisher, Sterling North, Carl Sandburg, and Ernest Thompson Seton, along with two Bible stories, but not as they appear in the Bible, with its grand imagery and noble prose, but retold in the most pedestrian language, plus four fairy stories. There is no example of the essay. The Fifth Grade Reader in this modern series introduces the child to no famous writers whatsoever except as (in the manual for teachers) it suggests supplementary library books. Except for a story by Liam O'Flaherty, Howard Pyle's "Tom and the Treasure Chest," and John Ruskin's "The King of the Golden River," the Sixth Reader contains nothing that can be classified as literature.

Most school children in my generation read Ruskin's "The King of the Golden River," but we did not read it at twelve. We read fairy stories, to which it belongs, when we were seven, eight, nine, or ten at the latest, when we were reading *Alice in Wonderland*, *The Water Babies*, and contemporary stories for small children. At twelve, in upstate New York village schools, we were beginning to read passages from the great English classics, as written for adults.

A question is not only "*Can* Johnny read?" but "What makes him *want* to read?" And what makes any child want to read is not only information or a banal story about familiar things and types, but his awakening, if it ever comes, to the brilliance, magic, fancy, imagery, metaphor, rhythm, percipience, freshness, and originality of thought and expression, commanded by great masters of prose and poetry.

Superb writing exists at many levels of comprehension. Nothing is simpler than some of the lyrics of Shakespeare. His little description of winter beginning "When icicles hang by the wall," mostly written in monosyllabic nouns and verbs, in simple ab-ab-cd-cd verse, contains only one phrase unknown, orally at least, to most eight-year-olds. But there is all the difference in the world between this lyric, or "Under the Greenwood Tree," or "Where the bee sucks, there suck I," and what a textbook hack or anyone else could compose of the same words. These lyrics are haunting, evocative, memorable, beautiful.

And children, even not very bright children, have an extraordinarily sensitive aesthetic sense. The worst thing one can do to them is to blunt it by banal reading. The British novelist Arnold Bennett remarked in one of his diaries that a writer should never read poor or mediocre literature. Neither should anyone else, especially a child, whose taste is formed very early.

Children also have a natural moral and ethical sense that responds very faintly to the "Now, be a good boy" precept, but is stimulated by examples of the great virtues. The old Readers consciously set about morally to influence children by what they put before them to read. I have not found the word "sin" in any modern reader (and suspect that it is falling out of the language), but one frequently encounters sin and sinfulness in the stories of the old ones, sin being anger, hatred, greed, gluttony, intemperance, cruelty, wrath, sloth, disloyalty, hypocrisy, dishonesty, untruthfulness — the real, big sins.

Yet the emphasis in the old Readers is not on sin but on virtues: Courage, honesty, charity, truthfulness, purity, industry, lovingkindness, justice, patriotism, family affection, and fidelity.

The editors of the old Readers set before school children, whether by story, essay, or poetry, the examples of great and illustrious men of refined and elevated character. Here Henry V, Shakespeare's noble and winsome King, prays that he act as the instrument of God. Here, in the conversation between Cassio and Iago, from *Othello*, Cassio inveighs against drunkenness. Here, Lord Chatham, in the British Parliament, makes his courageous and unpopular plea for the removal of British troops from the American Colonies, and Patrick Henry before the Virginia Convention setting forth the condition of the colonists and their experiences with the British government draws the logical but regrettable conclusion "Gentlemen may cry peace, peace, but there is no peace. . . . Is life so dear or peace so sweet as to be purchased at the price of chains and slavery?" And the child reader thus learns that there was more in the war for American Independence than black or white generalities, and that brave, just, and thoughtful Britons understood the American cause when many Americans were fainthearted.

Here Jefferson reveals his chivalrous understanding and admiration for the defeated Indian chieftain, Logan; here, in a scene from Schiller's *Wilhelm Tell*, the Swiss mountaineer fighter for liberty defies the foreign tyrant, accepting his challenge to put his arrow through an apple on the head of his cherished son, while the boy stands proud and confident in his father.

Courage is the ever-recurrent theme, courage in behalf of liberty and justice.

To what ignominy in these crumbling pages are liars, cheats, cringers, and hypocrites exposed! With what tenderness are deeds of compassion related! With what contempt are ingratitude and infidelity castigated! With what ardor are examples of generosity, and loyalty presented — by writers who could make words strengthen the spine, soften the heart, awaken delighted laughter, evoke penitent tears, sting into action, restrain from wrath, shame out of selfishness, soothe from grief.

The editors of the old Readers were patently intent to use great literature as a means to building character. How little of that appears in the Readers of today! Even the great American heroes, if they appear at all, are bloodless, namby-pamby, without vitality, pluck, or distinguished ideas. They do not come to life. Nor do the new texts allow them to speak for themselves. They talk about them, restating their ideas in language that would turn the stomachs of the originals. The standards of conduct depicted in the stories are vague. A child has to be well along in his reading lessons before he encounters even the words "love," "loyalty," "honesty," because they are "abstract." Nor does he meet with vivid, convincing examples of these virtues. Sin is out, because children are not sinful, but (and quite logically) so is virtue. The children depicted in modern Readers live in an uncharted ethical miasma of being "happy," engaging in do-it-yourself pursuits, imbibing vague (and often extremely inaccurate) bits of history and biography, with nice fathers and mothers in the background, who display no virtues beyond being kind and indulgent to their little ones.

No one can accuse America of neglecting the physical needs of children. They are washed and bathed, fed balanced diets, dressed comfortably and becomingly, and indulged in much they do not need at all. But they are not offered the bread that nourishes strong characters or shining minds. The fare produces mental and spiritual rickets.

Well, J. Edgar Hoover repeatedly comes up with new figures on juvenile delinquency. Recently he reported that in 1955 one out of every thirty-five youths between the ages of 10 and 17 were arrested, that 42 per cent of all persons arrested for major crimes are under the age of 18, and half of that number under 15 — this in the epoch of universal "education." There is little to hold them back except the repeated slogan that "Crime Does Not Pay."

Ours has also been called "The Age of Treason" — an age in which persons in all countries, including high intellectuals, simply do not know to what they are loyal, to what they have duties, or the meaning and responsibility of an oath.

"So," I suppose some reader will say, "you want us to go back to the nineteenth century and reintroduce McGuffey!"

Certainly I do not. We live in a different time. The nineteenth century was an age of great parliamentarians and orators, whose speeches and writings were often overloaded with rhetoric, and who greatly influenced the literary taste of the day. The old Readers, along with the immortal passages, abound in others by writers whose sentiments are sicklied o'er with a sentimentality unendurable today. By refined modern taste, much in the old Readers is overwritten and overspoken.

But most of the material in the modern Readers is not written or spoken at all. It is so unimaginative and indiscriminating that it would not pass the critic of a provincial newspaper if reviewed as literature — which it never has been! In fact, the writers of modern textbooks are the *only* writers who escape the critics, though their works go through more editions than those of many American authors of national and international renown. Their readers are captive children whose brains are being flattened and imaginations bled by streamlined reading created by conformist streamlined literary WPA's whose notion of literature is a "project."

Must we go on like this? Has the educational bureaucracy so intrenched itself that laymen, parents, taxpayers, or dissident teachers (who number legions) dare not raise a few pertinent questions or offer, without malice, advice based upon the long experience of the race?

Can we not again enlist distinguished thinkers and writers in Readers? It would not be necessary to go back to the nineteenth century — though why should we skip the human wisdom and experience of any epoch? Socrates, Pericles, Aeschylus, Tacitus, Isaiah, Amos, Proverbs, Ecclesiastes, Jesus, and Paul are not "dead."

Shakespeare is neither dead nor "old-fashioned." Revivals of the immortal bard flourish from Moscow to Iowa. Must a ten-year-old first learn of Shakespeare on a TV set? Cannot a twelve-year-old learn of Jefferson from Jefferson himself?

Can he not absorb courage from Ernest Hemingway's *The Old Man and the Sea* and the wondrous tales of William McFee? If his interest in freedom is unlikely to be aroused by Lord Chatham, can it not be stimulated by Winston Churchill, who put a nation on its feet by words, and received the Nobel Prize for *Literature?* Must he first learn of early New England sailors and whalers from the film version of *Moby Dick?* Are not some of the whimsical short stories of Sinclair Lewis ("Little Bear Bongo") worthy of a Reader for ten- to twelve-year-olds? Must Walt Disney be a better moral educator than the educators? Is there nothing in E. M. Forster or Somerset Maugham that can be excerpted for the young?

Would a child resist the childlike beauty of some of the earlier poems of Edna St. Vincent Millay? Or the descriptions of Paris by Scott Fitzgerald? Or of Bohemian immigrants by Willa Cather? Or of nature by William Henry Hudson?

There are passages in the works of most great or distinguished writers and statesmen that are of limpid simplicity. Even this cannot be said for some of the reading texts in use. There is a difference between simplicity and simpletonism.

Names come to me at random, but the old fact, the eternal problem of great writers, reasserts itself in every generation, in all time, as long as there shall be writers, who are artists and seers. All life is struggle, and the essence of struggle is between good and evil. Not a single great and enduring work of art, as expressed in words, has failed to meet the challenge of this struggle. The greatest literature is *moral.*

Give the child great literature and without preachment he will discern between good and evil, and yearn and learn to do well.

"Reading maketh a full man," said Bacon, a contemporary of Shakespeare.

Reading maketh a *good* man, thought William McGuffey.

"Train up a child in the way he should go: and when he is old he will not depart from it," says Proverbs 22:6.

And whatever changes, these truths abide.

Respect for Law Begins at Home

SOME TIME AGO an internationally famous psychiatrist told me the following story, which I recall in his own words.

"Two well-to-do middle-class people, the father a business executive, came to consult me about their only child, a nine-year-old son, who they declared was suffering from a serious 'compulsive neurosis' which led him to wield the scissors on everything in his home. He had slit the furniture coverings, demolished the draperies, cut his mother's best dresses to ribbons, and finally begun on his father's shirts and suits. The cutting mania had begun some three months before their visit to me.

"I inquired whether he had previously displayed destructive tendencies. They said, 'not really,' but confessed that in a temper he would sometimes break dishes or ornaments around the house. I inquired what they had done about it, and they replied that they had both 'reprimanded him very severely,' but that scoldings, and even his mother's pleas and tears had no effect.

"I said I would like to see Bobby, but not in my office, and not with his knowledge that I was a psychiatrist or a doctor, and they suggested that I drop in for a social call when the boy was at home and I could talk with him as a casual family acquaintance.

"This was arranged and I saw Bobby for an hour or so and drew him out without resistance on a number of subjects — his schoolwork, his teachers, his reading matter, and his favorite television programs.

"The next day I had a conference with his parents, who eagerly inquired what I thought was wrong with Bobby, whether I would take his case, and how prolonged I thought the treatment might be.

"I told them that I did not think there was anything seriously wrong with Bobby, and that I would take his 'case' provided his parents would cooperate fully, which they instantly agreed to do.

" 'I am not sure you will,' I countered. 'Has Bobby ever been punished?'

"Again they reiterated that he had often been severely reprimanded. 'Doctor, I have *wrestled* with that boy,' the father almost wept.

" 'And it hurt you and his mother a good deal more than it did Bobby,' said I. 'Well now, you, Mr. X, go home and tell Bobby you've had all you intend to take. Tell him the next time he cuts or otherwise destroys anything in the house, you are going to lick the pants off him. Don't hide the scissors. And then when he starts again being Jack-the-Ripper, do so — give him a *hiding.*'

"The parents were flabbergasted. They were, in fact, outraged. 'Do you think *that* will cure Bobby?' the mother said scornfully. 'No one has *ever* lifted a hand to that child. We believe in love.'

" 'So do I believe in love,' I replied, 'but love is a two-way street, and as far as children are concerned, it includes respect. Bobby is a perfectly normal boy. He is bright, healthy, and full of energy. But he has no respect for either of you. And because he has none for his own father and mother, he also has none for his teachers or any other authorities.'

" 'But why,' moaned his mother, 'does he do such things? There must be a *reason*.'

" 'He does them to assert his own power — his ego. He does them to challenge you. There is nothing psychologically abnormal about that. All children challenge authority. What is abnormal in this situation is that he gets away with it. He knows that you are bigger and stronger than he, and that you are highly respected in the adult community. Nevertheless, he, little Bobby, can destroy your possessions, drive you frantic, reduce you to helplessness.'

" 'If I give him, as you recommend, a hiding, will that stop him?' the father asked.

" 'Not the first time. The warning that you will do so will roll right off him. He won't believe you. Then when you do it, he will be furious — he will hate you for the time being, and he will destroy something again, partly out of revenge, partly to test whether you really mean business. Then lick him again. I think it will take three lickings — then he will stop.'

" 'And hate his father,' said the mother bitterly.

" 'Not unless you side against his father, and weep over Bobby, and pet and comfort him. If you stand by your husband your son will develop a healthy respect for his old man. And he *wants* to respect him. All children *need* to respect their parents.'

"The father followed my advice. The mother stood by her husband and stoically repressed her feelings, and Bobby's 'complex' was cured. It took quite some time, because Bobby had never been told *NO*, in the firm intention to make the command stick. If he had been treated with loving firmness from infancy, he probably might never have had to be spanked. Nine is a late age to be spanked. Nine is a late age to begin disciplining a child. But better late than never. For if Bobby had gone on as he was doing, society would eventually have disciplined him, in a really cruel way."

This story was told in a discussion of juvenile delinquency. My eminent friend, on the staff of a famous mental hospital, expressed himself very strongly on the cause of juvenile crime, and its link with psychotic disturbances. He argued as follows:

A child's first encounter with "law" is in his own home — with the rules and regulations established by his parents, and especially by his father, who initially appears to the child as all-powerful. The child knows that his father is the support of the family and the source of its well-being — his role in the young mind is rather like that of God. A child must know his father to be kind, loving, and beneficent. But he must also see him as Justice — as lawgiver and law-enforcer. The mother is naturally the child's intercessor. But every home needs a father; it is very difficult for a mother to play the dual role of judge and comforter.

The child's attitude toward his mother should be that of the protected and protecting. Boy children especially should early learn to do things for mother — to run to fetch her something she wants, to help her in little ways, to make her smile, to reciprocate, in short, her protectiveness. And this is one of the first laws of the home that the father should lay down and enforce — that the children treat his wife and their mother with gentleness, respect, and consideration — that they are obedient to her training. For by this the child knows that his father loves her, and the love of his parents for each other is the very foundation of his emotional security. Children are all instinct. They know that if their parents love and respect each other, they, the children, are also assured of love.

The father must, however, represent the final authority — he must, as the saying is, "lay down the law."

Laws for children are, or should be, very mild, and represent a hierarchy of lesser and greater thou shalt and thou shalt nots. Children should never be punished for things that merely cause inconvenience to adults — though these can also be reduced by inculcating good manners, for which the most effective instruments are praise, pride, and example.

But there must be other laws in the home that actually correspond on a small and childish scale to the laws of civilized states. Lying, stealing, destroying property, indecently exposing oneself, malicious assault — these are forbidden by every legal code, and their infraction in the home should meet a stern and instantaneous reaction. For if no code is enforced in the home, by that beneficent Godlike authority who is Papa, the child grows up "lawlessly," unprepared to recognize or obey the laws of society.

Bobby, for instance, was guilty of what, in legal terms, is called "vandalism." The laws of society — of the state — did not touch him because his offense was committed in his own home, under the protection, actually, of his parents. But the next step in Bobby's career would have been an extension of that vandalism. It goes on all the time — the breaking of windows, slitting of automobile tires, defacing of walls. Then its perpetrators become "delinquents." Similarly, a child who kicks his mother without encountering "the wrath of God" will kick his teacher next, and go on to worse brutalities. It is ridiculous to expect a child, as he enters teen age, with the violent exaggerations of instincts and urges that so often accompany puberty, to suppress them in obedience to the laws of society when he has never become conscious that there is such a thing as law, enforced by the first authorities he ever encounters — his parents — and by the next authorities — his teachers.

Children learn self-control by initially being controlled. Much of morality or immorality is habit, and all of civilization rests on the cultivation of inhibitions. Few children — there are some exceptions — are *naturally* good or bad. They become one or the other according to how the twig is bent. Even training in manners, superficial as that may appear, influences the inner development of a child. A class, for instance, that stands up when teacher enters the room, is making a gesture that implies respect, and the mere gesture helps put the pupils in a frame of mind to accept the teacher's authority. The first and most basic training, without which all further education will fail, is in *deportment*. My friend repeated, "If a child is permitted to be rude to his father or mother or teachers, he will become a rude youth and a rude man, and crime is only the ultimate expression of a rude mind and soul."

My friend went on to express himself on the relation between crime and insanity, remarking that both were on a serious increase in America.

"In the hospital where I serve," he said, naming a nationally famous one, "we have every variety of mad people — paranoiacs, schizophrenics, manic-depressives, melancholics, etc. In some few cases their derangements have a physical or congenital cause, but such are in the minority. The majority are just people who have lost control.

"And how do we cure them — and we do cure very many? We put them under control, like children in a nursery. Every hour of their day is mapped out in strict routine — rising hour, breakfast, occupational therapy, lunch, rest, sports, bath, dressing for dinner, bed — rather like a very strict, old-fashioned boarding school. Usually, during the first few days they rant and rave rebelliously, but they learn very quickly, crazy though they are, that Father's word is law — Father, in their case being the doctors and staff — and that the law will be enforced. No good, modern mental hospitals put people into painful straight jackets or abuse them in any way. But we have other nonpainful ways of wrapping up violent cases so they cannot harm themselves or others. And as they come to accept control they begin, gradually, to regain self-awareness and self-control. When they can discipline themselves and recognize and control their illusions they are cured.

"Many suffer from mental breakdowns for reasons that might induce the same condition in almost anyone. But I am convinced from long experience with thousands of cases that others would never see the inside of a mental hospital if they had ever learned self-control through being properly controlled as children. We have to start them all over again — in a nursery."

Though this conversation occurred several years ago, I have never forgotten it. My friend's remarks on juvenile delinquency ran counter, of course, to the prevailing notions of its cause, which is largely attributed to physical environment — to poverty, slums, inadequate recreational facilities for youth, the evil influence of some popular forms of reading matter (horror comics, for instance), and the violence depicted in some radio and television programs and movies.

I would not write these off as contributing factors. I am no apologist for poverty or slums. But the facts about juvenile delinquency and crime do not jibe with this explanation. Juvenile crime is on the increase in every social class and in every type of community — in country towns where no children need play in the streets, in expensive suburbs, in beautifully laid-out government housing projects, where, in fact, vandalism is very common, and it has been steadily increasing along with a general rise in the standard of living. It is far worse than it was in the depression years.

Although much visual matter available to minors is coarse, violent, and evilly suggestive, and requires greater public regulation, there have always been panderers of pornography. But responsible parents saw to it that such literature did not fall into their children's hands, and that tastes were cultivated which would contribute to their rejecting it if it did.

What can clearly be equated with increase in delinquency is the accompanying relaxation of discipline in home and school, where the child and teen-ager is allowed freedoms incompatible with his immature responsibilities and capacities of judgment. Granted that the moral and intellectual disciplines of forty years ago were often so strict as to be oppressive and creative of rebellion; that the old-fashioned teacher was sometimes tyrannical and despotic without being benevolent; and that at no time have all, perhaps most, parents been loving, kind, just, and still, where necessary, stern, the situation is not improved but worsened by standing relationships upside down — by firing a teacher who punishes a child, but doing nothing to a child (or his parents) who kicks a teacher!

Respect for law — for rules of conduct and deportment — begins in home and school, or it does not begin at all. And lawlessness is a self-perpetuating, ever-expanding habit.

Elderly
Reflections

"There Is a Time"

"THERE ARE," I recently remarked at a party, "distinct advantages to growing old."

The immediate reaction to this remark was amusing — and typical. The gathering was largely composed of people in the early and later forties, with a sprinkling of the young married set. These now protested vigorously, "How do you know!" one exclaimed "Why do you *even think* of old age!"

This haste to reassure me was affectionate, I thought, and even flattering. But it completely missed the point that I was not *complaining* of growing old. On the contrary, I was speaking aloud something that had often crossed my mind.

Apparently, I thought to myself, there is something *painful* about this subject. One oughtn't to *admit* one's age. It is as though one unnecessarily conjured up a melancholy specter, or brought disastrous personal news into a gay party. But what I was thinking, and had started to say, *was* news to me — good news, unexpected news — namely, that I am looking *forward* to being old!

A white-haired lady, with many quizzical humorous lines around her still keen eyes, smiled upon me. "You are right," she said quietly. "There are advantages. But why anticipate? Old age hardly begins before sixty."

"I suppose," a young physician interjected, "that you feel *wiser* than the young. That's the advantage."

So now they thought I was *flaunting* my experience and years! That wasn't it, either. "Old" people can be just as silly as the young. And though youthful silliness can be delightful, mature silliness is abhorrent. People are wise or unwise in their years, I thought. There is the wisdom of the child, of the youth, of the man or woman — and of the old. There are satisfactions in each period of life — satisfactions and frustrations, pleasures and pains.

> *To everything there is a season, and a time for every*
> *purpose under heaven:*
> *A time to be born and a time to die; a time to plant,*
> *and a time to pluck up that which is planted; . . .*
> *A time to weep, and a time to laugh; a time to mourn,*
> *and a time to dance; . . .*
> *A time to get, and a time to lose; a time to keep, and*
> *a time to cast away; . . .*
> *He hath made every thing beautiful in his time . . .* *

How could I express what was forming in my mind about the later years of life? Wherein did I find pleasurable contemplation of them?

Was I thinking of those insurance advertisements that hold out the joys of retirement in an idyllic cottage in a mild climate, with a modest but certain check coming in regularly, and nothing to do but "rest"?

---

* Ecclesiastes 3.

The insurance check is not to be scorned. There is always the material problem of old age. One has to have saved something — to have *some* resources — to face old age with that equanimity which is in itself one of the advantages of growing old. But a life without further effort?

Perish the thought! I know (as much as I know anything) that as long as I live I shall write. If public and publishers cease to be interested I shall write anyhow, perhaps only because formulating one's thoughts comes to be a habit impossible for most writers to abandon — a kind of personal luxury. I once knew a very famous writer who always wanted to write poetry. When he died the drawers of his writing desk were full of poems, written in the last two years of his life, poems he had never even tried to publish, although anything from his pen, good, bad, or indifferent, commanded a price commensurate with his fame. I thought affectionately of him pacing the floor, composing in his mind complicated rhyme schemes, searching for exactly the right word (the word to make more words dispensable, because poetry is of all writing forms the most economical), writing poetry, as he told his secretary, "because the exercise invariably improves one's *style*."

I hope I shall never cease to learn. Delightful the story of the octogenarian Mr. Justice Holmes, whom young Franklin D. Roosevelt found reading Plato.

"Why, Mr. Justice?"

"To improve my mind, young man!"

When all effort ceases, one is not old. One is dead — maybe walking around on one's feet.

Our government's Social Security measures, designed to aid the old, have a feature that I find unjust and inhumane. An employee contributes his share through his working life in the promise of an income at 65. The catch in getting it is that he must practically stop working altogether, for even if he earns below what he can live on, the pension will not be paid out.

Few people can do, or earn, as much at 65 as they can at 50, or even 60. But nearly everyone wants to have some small place in the world of work and usefulness as long as his health permits. I cannot see that it is the government's business or right to withhold an earned pension from the old who can still earn part of their living, and may need to do so. The government does not, incidentally, withhold the pension from those who have inherited a fortune!

But the luxury of such late efforts, as I contemplate them for myself, is that they are performed without external ambition, without desire for praise or fear of blame. One joy of old age is that in it we lose such ambitions — the ambition for applause, recognition, popularity; the fear of an endangered "career"; the pain of the slight. The world of such ambition belongs, in the nature of things, to the young. It is a necessary spur for most of us. But it is unseemly for the old to try to push the young out of the world's path, and it is also burdensome to try to do so. In youth and middle years one's contemporaries are not only one's friends; they are also one's rivals. In old age we remember our own youth and try to help the young to realize the ambitions we have ourselves abandoned. And this brings a new, refreshing form of freedom.

Perhaps we have grandchildren!

If we love children, what a luxury, and how different the relationship from that with our own!

How much more tolerant we are bound to be of their faults. We identify ourselves with our own children in an often painful way. What mother has not known the anguish of her child's wrongdoings? The humiliation of the conference with the teacher about her child's unsatisfactory deportment or inattention to his studies? The wakeful night, listening for the return of the sixteen-year-old daughter; the light turned on and off for the glance at the wrist watch or bedside clock — 2 A.M., 3 A.M. — there she is, at last, but the dance was to be over at midnight, and *where* has she been, and *what* has she been doing?

The years with a beloved son, going through an especially violent adolescence — scrape after scrape — the pitying eyes of one's friends, the well-meant advice: "Don't you think you ought to have him *psychoanalyzed?*" or, "I tell you, you spoil him!"

Always that identification: What is wrong with *me?* I don't know how to bring up my own children! It's my *fault.* The inner anxiety, and shame.

But Sue and Joe grew up. Sue married happily. Joe abruptly at 20 became, it seemed, an absolutely different character. You thought he'd never get through high school; then, suddenly, he found an objective for his life — in one of the sciences, arts, crafts, or industries — and the professor's or employer's smiling statement: "We are impressed by your son. He will make his mark." Delirious joy! (*Too* delirious!)

Now Sue and Joe are worried about *their* children — about Mary and Dick. But you, their grandmother, are not worried a bit. They will turn out *all right.* It's not *your* job to discipline them anyway. You can just love them — you will be the one to "spoil" them, from, I hope, a discreet distance. What luxury!

Then — the love of old age.

The earlier turbulence is gone — the quarrels, the fears, the bitternesses, the secret tears. The time John became involved with the "other" woman, and you went to see the lawyer — that was the worst time, worst of all, twenty years ago. Today you can hardly remember what she looked like! How dear now is his beloved face! How dear the very things that once irritated you! The comfort of his mere presence — the turning toward him in the night and the arm he puts around you, protectively, unconsciously, without waking. The habits and tastes that are as mutual as a shared bed — the foods you both like; the people; the landscapes. The wish of neither to change the other — not one bit. The being loved for exactly what one is, for better or worse, richer or poorer, in sickness or health. Not to have to explain oneself any more! It takes so *long* to get to be married! But what a luxury is a ripened marriage!

It is said contemptuously that the old enter a "second childhood." I would not say it contemptuously. As one grows older, one becomes aware, like the child, of how little one knows, and with this awareness comes again the sense of wonder of the child. In the years of striving one tends to lose touch with nature. With eyes on some material goal one has eyes for little else. A raise of pay is more exciting than the rising of the sun; an unhappy love affair makes one deaf and blind. As one grows older one's ears are not so good, but, curiously, one often hears more. One listens to music with receptive calm, untroubled by harassments of the mind. A beautiful day comes like a lovely gift. One suddenly notices again, as one did as a child, the form of a leaf, the contour of a tree, the fragile loveliness of the white cosmos, the bronze blaze of the Michaelmas daisies; the colored pattern of a city street; the stars. As one's sight dims, one seems to recover one's eyes.

As we grow older, we put our "houses in order." It is rather like a fall cleaning. What have we that we no longer want? Sue has always adored a ring that once you cherished. Joe's wife admired that necklace the last time she was here.

Give them away! Give away everything that has come to mean little to you.

In middle age we tend to accumulate. As we grow older we tend to get rid of things. We cease, for instance, to look for new friends, but all the dearer become the old and tested ones.

We reduce our "standard of living" by artful elimination. The house or apartment may prove too large — for need, comfort, or care. But in less space we retain familiar things, happily the most beautiful things, and for everyday use.

We reduce or eliminate certain activities — not necessarily because we don't feel up to them physically, but because a different order of priorities has formed itself.

We do many things most of our lives largely because others do them, as part of a social life that develops around us. Do I really *want* to go to Mrs. Weaver's cocktail party? Or see the much-talked-of play — and afterward struggle for a taxi? Or would I rather stay home, and finish the book I am reading? Maybe I feel like the party or the play. I haven't retired from the world yet, nor hope ever wholly to do so. But I find home more entertaining than I used to.

Thus one wins more "time." I already find myself with more time, not because I am not working as much as I ever did, but because I'm not playing at things and in ways I no longer care about.

All my life I have had what one might call an unhappy love affair with the world — its charms and achievements; its wars, revolutions, injustices. Now I know that the world got along without me for a long time and will do so again. Once I was very eager to reform my fellow men and their institutions. Now I am more concerned to understand them.

As one grows older, certain mental changes occur. The mind, of course, is the last part of oneself to grow old. Normally it reaches full maturity at about sixty. Some qualities diminish — for instance, the great quality of creative imagination. But the powers of judgment and discrimination increase rather than diminish, as long as the mind is actively used. One is less inclined to accept the popular intellectual idols and political slogans of the times; more inclined to contemplation. By sixty — and particularly, perhaps, in this century — one has lived through so many modes of thought that one ought to be able to distinguish the transient and superficial from the lasting and firmly rooted: the notion from the idea.

"But" (the young will make the mental reservation, without articulating it, being tactful) "you just, in the nature of things, are facing illnesses. After all, people die."

That's odd, too. I remember when I was afraid of developing some fell disease. (What will happen to my family!) Now I never think about it. I'd *like*, of course, to fall down like an old tree, when my sap has run out. But, as one grows older, one lives more as children do, in the present. One is not striving after the future and therefore not anticipating either its possible achievements or probable pains. Whatever may befall won't cripple one "for life." One isn't going to drag out "one's best years" in a bed or a wheelchair. Maybe one won't drag them out at all! Who knows?

Today is precious. My life *now* is happy and fruitful. *Maybe*, I will go again this spring to Europe and the Middle East. Or India (I've never been in India). Yes, I will take that limited number of lectures this winter (God willing). But *today* I'm going to finish this article.

And — thanks for listening, if anyone has. As I started to say — there are advantages in growing old!

"He hath made everything beautiful in His time."

"A Reason to Live and a Reason to Die"

In reading Whittaker Chambers' remarkable book, *Witness*, which better enables one to penetrate the mind of the genuine Communist than anything I have read, I came across this sentence in a passage wherein Chambers had been explaining and warning of the power of Communism over the human mind, conscious of crisis and longing for vision.

> *A man . . . peering upon a world in chaos finds in the vision the two certainties for which the mind of man tirelessly seeks: a reason to live and a reason to die.*

The sentence brought me up short, and I laid the book aside to think about it, and, at first, as a strictly personal challenge. Have I, in my lifetime, been "tirelessly seeking a reason to live and a reason to die"? Definitely not. Is that because I lack a seeking mind? I do not think so. Mine is a mind constantly questioning, challenging, weighing, doubting, looking for answers and being dissatisfied with most of them, including many most generally accepted.

But — a *reason* to *live*? My mind formulated an instantaneous answer: Life itself is a "reason to live." "My reason to live is because I *love* being alive."

Then I thought one could drop the last two words. "My reason to live is because I love."

Some reader is certain to say, "Oh, well, you have been lucky. You have a lot. Why shouldn't you love to live?"

Yes, I have been in some ways fortunate, especially in having had, on the whole, exceptionally good health. But I have known poverty, and had, I think, my full share of sorrows, cares, griefs, and frustrations, and one swift and very serious illness from which I did "nearly die." In that illness — a ruptured appendix and peritonitis before the days of penicillin — I was taken on a Christmas night from a Berlin hotel in a semi-coma from pain, and through the pain and sinking darkness, I remember saying to myself, "I am dying." Perhaps I was too ill to care. Nature, I think, prepares the mind to accept such a reality. It did not, I recall, frighten me. It appeared, rather, as a probable fact, a not uninteresting fact, a new experience — an experience, perhaps, of life in another habitat of consciousness. When, however, "I came to" — not out of the ether but into the consciousness that life, instead of poison, was coursing through my veins again, it was raining. I love rain. Two lines from Edna St. Vincent Millay's "Renascence" flashed across my mind: "I would I were alive again/To kiss the fingers of the rain." The glittering branch of an ice-robed tree moved across the window, and a bowl of autumn roses stood on a table and a pot of cyclamen on the sill. I was so glad to be back in this world of rain and sun and trees and flowers. After all, it's the only world I've ever known, and I just love it!

When I say "To be alive is to love," or "The reason for living is loving," I don't mean "love" in the limited sense it seems to have come to have— sexual love, or mother love, or love of humanity, in all of which there is pain as well as joy. (I don't know that I *do* love "humanity" much, especially in the abstract. I only know that I belong to it.) But I mean the love which sings hymns in the praise of things.

Sometimes I think (and I imagine I have written this before) that people actually have "taken leave of their senses." We can see, hear, taste, smell, and touch, and these senses are not only the primary means of self-protection but the source of greatest delight. It is through the senses that we receive our first impressions of the world, and make our first discriminations — between beauty and ugliness, bitter and sweet, scent and odor, smoothness and roughness, music and noise, and the higher the cultivation of the senses, the more refined and cultivated the person.

The senses are cultivated by use. The painter trains himself better to see, the musician to hear, the craftsman to touch, the chef to taste and smell. The expression accompanies and follows the training. But there is an artist in us all, otherwise artists would have no audiences. The extent to which we develop the artist in ourselves measures the extent to which we appreciate not only art but *life*.

The cultivation of the senses is intimately related to cerebral processes. People with blunted senses do not "make *sense*." "Vision" is an intellectual extension of the eye. A prophet is a "seer." Logic strives to arrange thoughts in an order. But from whence comes the idea of order? Obviously, it seems to me, it originates from *observation* of order, of an order not created by man, but of which man is an organic part — an order into which we are born.

I love life because I am conscious of my existence in an order which is sublime. My "reason to live" is to strive to recognize, accept, cooperate, and serve that order, and thus help to fulfill the law of Nature, Creation, God. And since that order encompasses my death, in organic nature, the acceptance gives me sufficient "reason to die."

Over and over again these days, we hear the phrase, "The world is in chaos." But "the world" is *not* in chaos.

I have been observing the world for a long time, and I wish to report that the world is in perfect order and always has been. In the many years during which I have been living, and admiring it, this planet has never failed to turn on its axis with exact mathematical certitude; the sun has never failed to rise and set; the blue star Arcturus has always appeared in exactly the same relationship to the constellation of the Bear; the Pole Star has never gone on a rampage to distract the mariner. An acorn has always produced an oak, and not an elm; sown wheat has produced wheat and not barley; the cosmos always comes up cosmos and not a Canterbury bell; Jersey cows bred to Jersey bulls bear Jerseys, not Holsteins; and the wild ducks always wheel southward at the same time.

The Bible is the greatest book ever written because it contains the most penetrating observations of the operations of natural law, the greatest warnings of what happens to men who defy it, and the most certain promises of happiness to those who accept and cooperate with it.

"Inventive man" has invented nothing — nothing "from scratch." If he has produced a machine that in motion overcomes the law of gravity, he learned the essentials from the observation of birds. If his gardens produce flowers and fruits once unknown, the flowers are all refinements by cross-fertilization of the original flowers of the woods and the fields, and the original fruits of the soil. The agriculturalist improves his fields only by observing and applying the inexorable facts of nature which decree that the organic and mineral matter taken from the soil by pastured beasts or as crops must be replaced or the land will become barren, and this without the slightest chance of failure.

Just laws are themselves only the codification of observed natural laws, and the best guide to ethics is observation of natural attractions and polarities. The aggressive invite aggression, the hateful, hate, the loving, love. We reap what we sow; we do not gather grapes from thorns or figs from thistles — the parables and teachings of Christ are almost all drawn from observations of nature, applied to human conduct.

Christ was the great life-lover, whose love of life encompassed his own innocent and sacrificial death, "that man might have *life* and have it more abundantly." His "reason to die" was his exact knowledge that being lifted up on the cross as the very symbol of love and life, he would draw all men unto him. Christianity is a *science* of conduct.

No, "the world" is not in chaos. *Men* are in chaos. They are in chaos because of disobedience, because of opposition to accepting their place in the natural order. Once man thought that the universe revolved around this planet. Eventually he was forced to recognize (in great offense to his pride) that the planet is a minor satellite. Now, modern man has been taught that *he* is the center of the planet. The most stuck-up, smart alec, and self-inflated of the animals, thinks he "knows better," thinks he knows it all.

Communism is the cult of those who think man created God, and not the other way around. That's the crux of the matter. That is what Whittaker Chambers has said in the opening chapters of *Witness*. And it is that, in the book, which has enraged not only the Communists but all the other smart alecs who share the basic premise of Communism, that it is man's duty to "change the world" in contemptuous disregard of its natural order. Those are the *sixth* column, the way-pavers for the Fifth.

But God's nature has a way of getting rid of disturbers of its order and peace. For "I, the Lord thy God, am a *jealous* God."

Yet, those who look for beauty, will find it; those who listen for the voice of truth, will hear; those who love will be loved; those who protect life will be protected by it — as long as the stars continue in their courses, the winds rise, and the rivers flow.

This is no longer something I "believe." It is something I *know*, confirmed by experience. When I have betrayed the belief and disregarded the knowledge, as I often have, I have been punished, not by courts but by inexorable effects of causes, and the punishment has never been unjust.

Life is a wonder and a miracle — life in all its phases, in fortune and misfortune. We take life, as we take our beloved in marriage, "for richer, for poorer, in sickness and health," and the first debt we owe to Life is a debt of gratitude.

I hate ingratitude more in a man than lying, thieving, babbling drunkenness.

Shakespeare was another of the great lovers and affirmers of Life — of *all* of Life, seeing, hearing, feeling, sensing its terrors, wonders, mysteries, revelations, grandeur. *Therefore*, he is the world's consummate artist. And *therefore*, he was able to retire from "the world" at a relatively early age and cultivate his garden.

"Because I have loved life, I know I shall love death as well," said Rabindranath Tagore.

He needed no further "reason to live, or reason to die."

The White Sofa

THE CHILDREN were furnishing their first real home, now that the baby had come and the little apartment they had taken near us, as a makeshift until they could find something more satisfactory, had become too small. The children are my son and daughter-in-law. They don't mind being called "the children" when there is no implication of their being minors and incompetent.

We had all looked for an apartment in overcrowded New York, which is rapidly becoming a city of homes for rich or poor only. On the unfashionable side of the city they had finally found an almost ideal apartment for their needs and income.

Some days later my son called up and reported, "Well, we've found a sofa! It was standing in a window, and we went right in and bought it."

"What's it like?" I asked.

"Oh, it's long, wide, and low. The covering is a nubbly white material. It will look swell."

"*White?*" I cried. "Have you gone *crazy? White* — in New York! You know what it means to keep house in New York — the soot — and *white* — and with a child in the house? Do you know what it will look like in no time — unless you are going to pay to have it cleaned every month? You say it's big, very wide. Well, it will jut too far into the room and look more like a white elephant than a sofa. I advise you to cancel the order — send it back — and what did you pay?"

He told me and I replied, "And it's too expensive also. Why in heaven's name didn't you shop around a bit?"

He answered that the sofa was already in the apartment, and besides, it was exactly what they wanted. "Goodbye," he said coldly, and hung up.

When I turned from the telephone, my husband (my son's stepfather) was flushed with anger. "You heard that?" I asked. "A white sofa! They haven't the sense they were born with."

"And you," said my normally loving husband, "haven't learned any sense about some things. You are the one who's crazy. Why don't you let the children alone? It's their home, not yours. It's their money, and for that matter they have a perfect right to make their own mistakes. Because of a darned sofa you are spoiling your relations with the children that normally could hardly be better. At this moment they're wishing you were in Timbuctoo, unless there's some place farther away."

I sat down, not quietly, but as though I had been pushed, and started to cry a bit. "So now you are *crying* over that sofa," my husband said with growing exasperation.

"No, I'm not," I sputtered. "I'm crying because I've been such a fool."

"Stop it," he said rudely. "But God forbid that you should ever have to live with the children!"

I sat there and brooded. My husband was absolutely right. I realized that from the moment the children had taken the apartment, I had been giving them unsolicited advice, and encountered, in my son in particular, a very stubborn resistance. It had started when he had announced — in comment on my suggestion that they look at some of the better auction galleries for nice pieces that could often be picked up inexpensively — "We don't *want* old furniture. We want the apartment contemporary — modern."

I realized that I had been steadily attempting to impose upon the children my own tastes. I don't like dark walls. I don't like green. I like traditional furniture — authentic eighteenth-century English and French if I can afford it, or good reproductions. I don't find most modern furniture comfortable. I detest "posture" chairs. I dislike side draperies. Curtains must draw. I don't like venetian blinds, which, when open, suggest to me prison bars. And, as one who has kept house for thirty years, I am conscious of such matters as durability and upkeep.

My son, I thought, had always loved his home with me. How often he had said, "Ma, I hope you never change a thing in this room. I like it exactly as it is. I wouldn't feel at home if you changed it."

He liked his *mother's* home. He liked the environment his stepfather and I have created for ourselves. He likes to think it's there. But it is not *his* environment. The children want to create their own. They don't want to live in an annex of yours, I said to myself, wondering how I could have been so incredibly stupid. So unbearably *bossy*.

I called up and apologized, saying I had been tired and cross. Eventually, when everything was in place, we were invited to dinner, my daughter-in-law watching me, I unhappily thought, rather anxiously. But the apartment was charming. The white sofa against a dark blue-green wall, was handsome. The furniture in all the rooms was well distributed, and in size and color harmonious. The apartment was expressive of the children. It was not remotely expressive of me — as I am now or as I was when I was their age. But it was becoming to them. I love to go there, enjoying the change from my own environment. And I don't have to live there.

"I don't have to live there." That thought echoing my husband's brought others in its train.

Suppose I did. Suppose things should work out that they would feel they must share a home with me. We love each other; our tastes in many things are highly compatible. But what would happen?

I have been mistress of my own home for many years. I am accustomed to a certain order and routine, partly established by my work. I am not an early riser, but a punctual one. I never lunch beyond a snack when I feel like it. I always dine at precisely the same time. I never receive visitors until after five o'clock in the afternoon. I am fixed in my ways.

They are good ways for me, and they happen, also, to conform with those of my husband. But he is my age. They are not the ways of my more helter-skelter children, always ready to change a date, change their minds, call up half a dozen people to come in for lunch or after dinner that very night, and outside necessary restrictions, live happily from day to day.

Some of my friends are their friends in whose homes we sometimes both find ourselves guests, and they seldom refuse an invitation to dinner at our house, even if there are no other young people. Youth has been emancipated from many old restrictions between generations. But in general their friends and interests differ from mine.

If we lived together, they or I would continually be making sacrifices and adjustments. We would start doing that, I am sure, with the utmost good will. But, in the end, one or the other would have to capitulate.

Nobody relinquishes his life easily. If I were to dominate, the family relationships of the children — to their children, and to their friends — would be immeasurably damaged. If I should capitulate, my life would end before its end.

If this were only a personal anecdote it would not be worth recounting. But it is not. How many women have written me on just this subject! Of the parent or "in-law" who has come to make a home with them and of the misery that has ensued. It is not that love is initially lacking. It is that love dies under the strain.

It was not always so — or not always to the same degree. In the world of Grandma Moses, one usually found a widowed grandmother or other relative, for whom there was "always room for one more." But that world was different. The home was not only a residence for a family gathered in their more intimate hours. It was a center of industry, in which young and old all had something useful and creative to do. The family lived in a community which was a visible extension of the families. Everyone knew everyone else for miles around and life was cooperative on a neighborly basis.

The farmhouses were uncomfortable by modern standards, but they were large. Few homes today have guest
rooms, and a guest means doubling up or turning a living
room into a bedroom by night. We have sacrificed space to
comfort, and by numerous labor-saving devices refinement
of taste has increased. The modern woman does not do as
much manual labor as her grandmother, but she is a more,
not less, conscientious housekeeper. Grandma cleaned house
in the spring and fall and what a scrubbing and rubbing and
polishing it was! But after that all it got for months was an
occasional lick and polish. Her granddaughter — with numerous mechanical aids — expects her home to be tidy and
immaculate every day.

Grandma served abundant meals but with little variety,
and, nobody having tasted anything else except "good solid
American food," everybody liked the same things. Her
granddaughter searches the magazines for new recipes — from
all the European countries and the Orient as well. So tastes
differ as they never did before, and especially between the
generations.

Grandma's recreations were homemade. Granddaughter's
are not. Even families consisting only of parents and their
minor children are coming to have more than one television
set and radio, in order that everyone should be pleased.

Life is lived more outside the home, in both work and recreations, so the harder to keep it together, the more cherished
is family intimacy, and the more disturbing the introduction
of another generation.

Why and under what circumstances do the elderly go to
live with their children?

I know of no statistical studies, but observation indicates
that it is rarely a question of money. Social Security, private
insurances, and industrial retirement pensions provide for the
old as never before. Usually one mate has died and the sur-

vivor is alone. And usually, he or she, has nothing to do. The combination of these leads them to seek the roofs and companionship of their adult children.

The fact that they are idle and have no work exacerbates the situation. The father of the family is away from nine to five. But the guest and housemate is home and underfoot all day. Grandma may baby-sit, but to care for a prolonged time for a lively two- or three-year-old taxes the physical strength of the youngest and heartiest. Grandparents who have brought up their own children are, with the rarest exceptions, unable to care for young children. It is simply too hard — far harder than regular work in a shop or office. And Grandpa is likely to be of no use at all.

But why are the elderly, able-bodied though they be, lonely and idle?

Here we come to the crux of the matter.

It has become a matter of policy that everyone should cease working at the age of 65, regardless of the individual condition. The Social Security laws encourage this by putting a premium on retirement. The pension schemes of industry require it. An employee is *automatically* retired.

Advertisements of insurance companies paint a rosy picture of the life of the retired beneficiary — the little house in Florida, Southern California, or some other mild climate; fishing, bridge, a leisurely game of golf. Institutions exist into which the elderly can buy their way — to live exclusively among others as old or older than themselves. The old are encouraged to cultivate hobbies — anything to get them out of the main stream of life.

There are, I have read, savage tribes of hunter-warriors who push the old over cliffs when they are no longer able to hunt and fight, these being the sole occupations — though this is not true of any primitive peoples of whom I have knowledge. Among Polynesians and Arabs, as among the

ancient Hebrews, the old are cherished for their wisdom.
They are the heeded counselors of the tribe and the community.

But in our society we are really pushing the old over the
cliff, in however "civilized" and "humane" a way.

The fact is that few who have been active all their lives
are capable of enjoying total leisure. Ours is not a leisure
society and the creative use of leisure is not something one
can begin to cultivate at sixty. We are a nation of workers.
And in this particular society and time those who are entirely
cut off from the world of work are cut off from life itself.

Our most vital contacts are with our fellow workers.
They are not all our age. In factory or office we work alongside young people just out of high school, vocational school,
or college, alongside middle-aged people, and older. It is a
vital community of work and interest. Even our social contacts are largely with people in the same or affiliated businesses
or professions.

Now, a man who has worked for many years in a business or
industry has reached "retirement age." The firm gives him
a dinner. The President rises and pays him a fulsome tribute
and presents him with a gold watch. His colleagues slap him
on the back and congratulate him. "Lucky dog, no more
having to get in by nine o'clock." He himself is, for the moment, elated. It's going to be swell to get up when one feels
like it, relax, have a vacation for the rest of one's life, do all
the things one has dreamed about!

But after a few weeks he realizes that he is on the shelf —
permanently. He calls up the fellows he used to lunch with
but they have other "business" engagements. He has an idea
for the business, as he often has had before, but there's no one
to communicate it to. Nobody cares.

On that day when he got the gold watch he felt fine. He
has made 65 with no serious disorders of health. He has been

accustomed to have people say, "You don't look a day over fifty." Now he feels as old as time. Nobody wants his accumulated experience. Nobody cares for his advice. Perhaps he's only been a shipping clerk, but what he didn't know about a shipping room nobody ever would. One day he meets an old colleague from the firm and asks, "Who heads the shipping room now?"

"They've got a young fellow in, and between us it's a mess. Wish you were back." And he thinks to himself, "Why did I have to quit?"

The people at the top don't quit — men of 70 and even 80 sit on boards of directors. United States Senators don't retire at 65. Self-employed professional men don't either. They work as long as they feel like it, which is usually until the day they die, relegating responsibilities, taking longer vacations, but becoming "deans" of their professions. Most Presidents of the United States have left office at an age over the retirement limit for hired employees, and retired "over-age" generals become counselors of corporations.

Industrial pension systems begin to operate against employees long before they reach the arbitrary retirement age. A man of fifty, looking for a job, is up against it, no matter what his competence, experience, and vitality. In 15 years the firm is going to have to retire him and pay him a pension, and they'd rather have someone who will be with them a longer time.

The automatic operation of retiring people at 65 would be arguable if there were a surplus of labor. But, except for a few industries, there is no surplus. Our economy is tight. Industries need and seek competent employees, but throw out still vigorous men and women for the purely arbitrary reason of age. Yet age is not measured by years. Nature does not equally distribute energy. Some people, it seems to me, are born old and tired while others are going strong at 70.

Many widowed people marry again after 60, and it's the most sensible thing they could do. Theirs are not marriages of romantic love, but usually contracted between old and affectionate friends, for comfort and companionship.

But in any case men and women who retain vital contacts with the world of work are less lonely than they would otherwise be. If they lunch with their fellow workers they can more easily endure dinner alone. If they leave their lonely dwellings every morning they can enjoy their quiet in the evening.

It is a great deal easier to retire with a companion at your side. Then you don't go home to park on the children! But the Social Security system militates even against such marriages. The widow who inherits, as a dependent, her husband's Social Security loses it if she remarries, though her new husband may also be dependent on Social Security.

Under the Social Security system, no one can draw upon it before 72 if he or she earns more than $1200 per year, so in hundreds of thousands of cases, to continue to work after 65 means to suffer a financial loss. Yet, if an elderly person has an income of $100,000 a year from investments or inheritance, he can draw his full Social Security at 65, and add it to his other income. Or continue to work and forget the deferred benefits. Social Security penalizes only *work*.

The twenties and thirties saw a revolt of youth.

The fifties should, I think, see a revolt of age.

Age needs an FEPC.

Age should demand, first, that pension and Social Security payments due at 65 or inherited should not be made dependent upon subsequent earnings and should not be revocable by remarriage.

Age should make organized protest against being put on the shelf for no other reason than an arbitrary date line. Many a man or woman who can no longer carry the burden of an accustomed job can perform with high efficiency during shorter hours or at lighter tasks. Industries can and should create openings for such persons who do not want to retire. But the older members of our society should resist being automatically pushed over the cliff.

Then we won't end up while still able-bodied and able-minded living with a white sofa, and being pests.

On
Public Affairs

The Affinity of War and Peace

UNESCO WAS SET UP by the United Nations to fight war through influencing the human mind. "Since all war begins in the human mind, it is in the human mind that it must be abolished," says the statute founding the agency.

Behind that statement is the idea that war can be abolished by the conversion of sinful (warring) man to good (peaceful) man. It poses the opposites — War and Peace — and demands man take a stand on the side of the angels. In this concept war is wholly evil and peace wholly good.

Were this so, war, I am convinced, would have faded away long ago. But it is possible to accept this thesis only if every other value and virtue recognized by the instinct and morality of mankind were made subservient to the one virtue: peace. Courage, honesty, truth, charity, generosity, self-denial are virtues, as cravenness, deceit, greed, and self-indulgence are vices. War is struggle, which the exercise of virtue by no means precludes, and struggle is inherent in life and growth. Thus, though peace is indivisible in our minds from virtue, virtue is not indivisible from struggle; and war, therefore, is not indivisible from peace.

Peace and war both represent man's paradoxical quest for the meaning of life, and for the creation and preservation of the societies fitting to his concept of that meaning and the aspirations arising from it.

There is a phrase in the Declaration of Independence which has always bothered me — as it bothered its author. It declares man's unalienable right to the "pursuit of happiness." It bothers me out of doubt whether happiness can ever be achieved by pursuing it. It would seem rather to be the earned though unanticipated and unsought-for by-product of pursuing other things, such as love, regarded more as giving than receiving; knowledge, as the route to wisdom; moderation, as a check on ambition and passion; truth, as the extension of perception; and work, as the more creative expression of one's nature. A man is happy when he is on relatively good terms with himself and his environment, and least happy when he feels called upon to ask himself concerning his happiness.

So, it seems to me, it is with peace. When people pursue peace and peace alone, they seem to end up only with appeasement — the giving away of their peace to others who are not pursuing it. When the world or a society is really at peace nobody even mentions the word "peace." Life seems to be unfolding more in harmony with natural law. Struggle, though constant, is restrained by commonly held assumptions of proper behavior. Even if brute force is invoked, combatants are restrained by common standards and restricted aims.

It is when peoples or classes no longer share any basic standards of virtue that the peace between them is threatened by destruction beyond hope of restoration. Then the struggle becomes fundamental. Under such conditions war may appear as virtue and peace as vice.

That is perhaps why the bitterest of wars have been religious wars, or quasi-religious wars in which secular ideas have taken on the compulsive force of a religion. The most dreadful European struggles have been of this sort: the great medieval crusades of the Christian passion against the Infidels; the terrible Thirty Years' War between Catholic and Protestant kings, which left Germany, its battleground, "with more wolves than men"; the Napoleonic Wars, which grew out of the French Revolution and were motivated by a passion to produce (or restrain) a new social order; the American Civil War, whose peculiar interest and passion were produced by the existence of slavery and horror at its extension; and World War II, whose passion was less against the Germans as a people than vehement aversion to the spreading of Nazism.

It is characteristic of such struggles that their lines are never wholly drawn along national frontiers, but are actually drawn in the minds of men. But the struggle that goes on in the human mind, in such great ideological crises, is not between war and peace, but between notions of good and evil, right and wrong.

Thomas Carlyle made the observation that "There is no passion of the mind of man but meets and masters the fear of death." War is not "murder," as some pacifists say it is. For murder is the removal of another person from life at no risk of one's own. It involves no concepts of virtue, and is usually the result of combinations of vices, while war is a struggle in which one's own life is as involved as the enemy's, and in which love and hate are equally engaged.

Men, therefore, paradoxically, fight their bitterest wars out of the deepest moral convictions or the most engrossing ideas. It is even true that in the human mind wars are often fought for "peace." Even Hitler had the idea that permanent peace could never be obtained until all the world was organized under one system and all force concentrated in a single hand, to police the world against further wars and rebellions. "The pacifist humane ideal would be excellent if first one man and one nation made itself master of the globe," he wrote.

The International Communists also believe that there can be no permanent peace until all the world is organized in one Marxian-Socialist system. In this mentality wars fought by "capitalist" powers are evil, but victorious wars fought by Communist states further such a world system and therefore bring closer a permanently warless world.

On the other hand, those who believe with equal passion that it is neither possible nor desirable to restrain all mankind within one rigid set of ideas or one single system — holding that the immense differences of tradition, talent, challenge, and opportunity among individuals and peoples point to diversity as a law of Nature and to totalitarianism of any kind as stagnation and decline — hope to achieve peace by legal and forceful restraints upon aggression. In their view only the certainty that aggression will be repulsed by overwhelming force is any guaranty of peace and liberty. But the forceful suppression of aggression is also war, though its object is the attainment of a warless world.

These and many other choices posed in the human mind are not choices between war and peace, but between good and evil. Millions of men who hate war have perennially decided that "it is better to die on one's feet than live on one's knees." Other millions, though deploring war, have exposed themselves and others to it out of conviction that the peace and prosperity of future generations depended upon the extermination by force of one social order and the creation of another, or the defense of one against another. Almost all men believe in the moral right and even duty of self-defense. The law exempts the individual from charges of violence when violence is employed in self-defense against an armed attack, and the United Nations seeks to outlaw "aggressive" war, not holding the defender equally guilty with the assaulter.

It therefore seems doubtful whether mere propaganda for "peace" accomplishes anything. War is one way by which men and nations defend what they consider good and resist what they consider evil, and it is not likely to be removed from the world — as long as men seek to distinguish right from wrong, which is their highest spiritual activity — unless an equivalent is found for it.

In domestic civilized societies struggle, though constant, is restrained from naked force (war) by processes of law and effective instruments of peaceful change. He who feels himself wronged does not seize a pistol or a crowbar, but takes his case to court. But were there no court in whose judgment he had a degree, at least, of confidence, he could find no justice except by naked force. Those in rebellion against phases of the social order fight for the minds of their contemporaries through political instruments. Even this does not preclude all violence, but since force is on the side of the law, the victory of defeat of ideas is aimed not at killing one's opponents but at changing the law and the lawmakers. As long as men have effective instruments, which their minds accept, for effecting or resisting change, they resort to such instruments. Conversely, they feel themselves justified in resort to force, in the absence of such instruments through which they can effectively struggle for what they conceive to be justice and the triumph of "right" ideas.

The problem of peace is not, therefore, the problem of eliminating the will to struggle. It is the problem of finding forms through which struggle can be canalized with the least destructive effects. All struggle is a *form* of war, bringing victories to some and defeats to others. None of it is painless.

But the unarmed struggles at least preserve that which man cannot restore once it is violently taken away — namely, the source of the struggle: life.

It is not, therefore, I think, the pursuit of "peace" which will lead us from war, but a deeper understanding of the nature of man, the recognition that struggle is a part of that nature, and that arenas that are not bloody battlefields must be provided for struggle. Perfect peace is total renunciation, and none except those rarest geniuses, spiritual saints, have ever found it this side of the grave.

Religion in American Life

AMONG THOUGHTFUL PEOPLE of various creeds, and even of no creed, one can discern a growing consciousness and conviction that the world crisis is, fundamentally, neither economic nor military, but moral, ethical, and religious.

It is, I think, an error to attribute this crisis to "Communism," or to believe that it has suddenly broken out as the result — for instance — of two world wars. That is putting the cart before the horse.

Communism was born in the middle of the nineteenth century, a very great century in many ways. Pre-eminently it ushered in the industrial age and the age of science, and rapidly advanced the belief in a materialistic and mechanistic universe and philosophy of life. Karl Marx was by no means out of tune with this age. Although he was a revolutionary radical, the basic assumptions of his work were the basic assumptions of his times, as they are still to a very great degree the basic assumptions of our own.

The belief that man is an economic animal, and that his life and culture are determined by the institutions of material production, were accepted by Marx's opponents as well as by his partisans. That the good life was the rich life — rich in material things — was the logical continuance of that line of thinking. It was also, then, logical to assume that if the owner-ship and control of the means of production could, by being divorced from the profit motive, assure abundance for all, all the evils in the world — both good and evil being eco-nomically inspired — would fade away, and man would re-turn, as it were, to a kind of idyllic condition, to a greatly improved Garden of Eden.

Marx, like many idealistic philosophers, reared an imposing logical structure on an assumption. For years it was the logical structure that was attacked by his opponents. It is only now, after actual test of his theories, that it is becoming daily more apparent that the fault lies in the assumption, not in the logic built upon it.

Man is, among *other* things, an "economic animal." But it is only at the most primitive level of existence that he is wholly, or even primarily, purely "economic." A man in cruel imprisonment, kept on rations approaching the starva-tion level, is likely to think chiefly of food. But human beings, even at the instinctive level, with a modicum of their diges-tive needs fulfilled, and with fairly adequate protection against the elements, in the form of clothing and shelter, have at least two other basic urges: the urge to be recognized as unique and apart, which is the *ego,* and the sexual urge.

These urges are not, in themselves, either good or evil. The economic urge — the will to prosper materially — is both the father of greed and the mother of invention and initiative. The ego can make a person into a glutton for power over his fellow men, or into their greatest benefactor. The sexual urge is both the parent of crime and the founder of the family; it can be sublimated at the highest level of love, into beneficence and art, and it can crop out in criminal insanity.

Human culture, as I see it, is created by the sublimation of these urges, which are parts of man's animal inheritance, into expressions compatible with his mental and spiritual growth, his personal happiness and joy, and his peaceable adjustment to the community.

All civilization rests upon the cultivation of inhibitions. So does all freedom and security. An uninhibited society is a savage society, a jungle, in which no one is either free or safe.

The function of law is to impose such inhibitions. The law is a series of thou shalt nots, and the weapon it wields is fear of punishment. But law is, itself, only the codification of existing states of consciousness and conscience. If the conscience of a society does not support the law, the law will not function.

But whence comes conscience?

We live today in a society that has the highest standard of living, and the widest distribution of the fruits of production, ever enjoyed by any human society in the history of mankind. Yet it shows at the same time an appalling crime record, and at every social level. Those entrusted to enforce the law are found to be on the payrolls of the lawbreakers, and government proves itself adept at circumventing the spirit, if not the letter, of what it would impose on the society it governs. Mutual mistrust is widespread. Loyalty is in question. A cynical frame of mind prevails that "every man has his price," and that behind every word and act is a mercenary or power-

seeking ambition. Parents struggle for any degree of authority over their children, and many even welcome the induction
of their sons into the army in the hope it will "teach them
some discipline." We find out that thousands of teen-agers
are dope addicts. And throughout our society is an undertow
of almost hysterical fear — fear of one's own state and of
other states, of Russia and of Communism, and, indeed, of
life itself. "Emotional maladjustment" reveals itself as the
most prevalent American disease, and while we make drives
against cancer and infantile paralysis the psychiatrists are
flourishing.

A society in such a condition is one showing symptoms of
disintegration, a society out of focus, because it has no frames
of reference, or basic loyalties to which the masses of its
people give natural, unconscious allegiance.

In a sound society, loyalties are inherent. They cannot be
established by loyalty oaths. Nor are they encompassed by
loyalty to a government, or a Constitution. They are loyalties
to a spirit which must constantly animate governments and
Constitutions if these are to retain their authority. And
authority can be exercised by a minimum of coercion only
if it ratifies the moral authority already present in the mind
and soul of a society — only if there is a strong and widespread conviction in the people themselves of what is right,
good, and permissible, and what is wrong, evil, and intoler-
able.

There is no historical example of any nation, tribe, or
society reaching and sustaining a high level of human culture, or even long maintaining its cohesiveness, without faith,
belief in, or acceptance of, the probability (I am putting this
as undogmatically as possible) that moral sanctions exist above
the human, the visible, the material, the tangible. As far back
as we have any records of man as man, we find him, and his

societies, concerned with the conviction that spiritual forces mold human life and conduct. And as far back as we have any records, we find man as a being of thought and spirit concerned with the question "Why are we here? What is the meaning of life and the purpose of existence?"

People and societies who cannot see any purpose in their existence beyond the material and the tangible must live chartlessly, and must live in spiritual misery, because they cannot overcome the greatest fact and mystery of human life, next to birth, which is death.

The answers cannot be proved by science — although modern science has already blown up the nineteenth-century assumptions of a material and mechanistic universe. The answers must come out of the spiritual experiences of man through the ages, the experiences which have produced the great religions.

A secular and materialistic age has scoffed at such experiences as "superstitions" or even as symptoms of madness, as though Jesus, Amos, or Francis of Assisi — or Gandhi — were less sane than, say, Harry S. Truman; or as though an experience of truth, born out of the most concentrated effort to shake off oneself and open every pore, every brain cell and nerve to messages from the unseen world, were not a real experience. The attitude is not itself "scientific," for it rejects evidence merely because it cannot explain it. The knowledge of the prophets, the seers, is just as "real," as (though much rarer, than) the knowledge that is won from the test tube or the telescope, though it is acquired through a different medium of insight.

It is my conviction that this country can only recover its poise and serenity when it refinds its religious loyalties, whether these be centered in the Jewish prophets or the revelations of Christ, and these loyalties come to suffuse the whole of its civilization.

This requires, among other things, a fundamental re-examination of our education. It has been secularized to the point that our schools not only shut out all religious or spiritual influences, but increasingly encourage agnosticism and atheism. A concept of the separation of church and state has grown up which, if it goes on, will finally result in our withdrawal from Judeo-Christian civilization altogether.

An education that does not admit even reference to religious experience and inspiration is a failure even of education in a quite narrow sense. No one can understand Western culture at all — the culture that is threatened as never in its millennial history — who does not understand its religious bases and the religious assumptions on which its very laws are based. No one unfamiliar with the major prophetic passages of the Bible can possibly read with comprehension much of the finest English literature, which is replete with biblical allusions. How in the world can any child make head or tail out of Lincoln's great Second Inaugural Address who does not understand the quotations, uttered without "quotes," that come directly from the scriptures, and the frame of reference in which they were originally made?

Can some of the greatest music of Western civilization be divorced from its inspiration — the great Passion music of Bach; the *Missa Solemnis* of Beethoven; the *Requiem* of Verdi; the *Elijah* of Mendelssohn? Must one be a Roman Catholic to recognize that the Mass is perhaps the most immortal work of art that Western civilization has ever produced?

Are some of the greatest pictures of the world merely decorative designs in form and color, to be taken apart from the spiritual atmosphere and faith which inspired them?

And is the function of education merely to train children for a job, and for the "correct social attitudes" (whatever these may be at the time), or is it also to cultivate their minds and their souls, to refine their senses and increase their sensibility to what is good, noble, and worthy to be emulated?

It is all very well to say these things should be "left to church and home." The church cannot function on the peripheries of a civilization. Even Communist states are willing it should drag out its existence divorced from the rest of life. The home has changed; in great cities it is reduced, for many families, into a functional apparatus for eating and sleeping in, not commodious enough to be a center of the child's life, which is increasingly spent in school, social activities radiating from the school, and in clubs and playgrounds.

The basis of all education must be training in character. It is character that determines the fate of societies — as the old Greeks knew when they said "Character is Destiny," as the poet Housman knew when he wrote, in *A Shropshire Lad*, apropos of Victoria's jubilee, "Get ye the men your fathers got, and *God* will save the Queen!"

A supposedly God-fearing people (ourselves) who take the lead in founding the United Nations, whose Presidents take the oath of office on the Bible, but who were afraid to open the San Francisco Conference with a prayer lest it offend the Russians, deserve the United Nations they have got.

A God-fearing people, sure of its moorings, has nothing whatever to fear from Communism. A nation spiritually adrift can be blown on the rocks by any high wind.

The Great Affirmative

WE WERE SITTING before the fire in the big room in our
Vermont farmhouse: my husband and I, a well-known writer
on the current scene, and two young instructors from a
famous eastern university. We talked about Communism,
and — apropos of the congressional hearings — why it man-
aged to gain and retain a hold on so many apparently bright
minds. In the course of the conversation I said that although
convinced that only a tiny minority of people anywhere were
believing Communists I missed a strong affirmation of another position. Anti-Communism is not enough, I said. One
must be *for* something, and believe in something else, as fer-
vently as Communists and other apostles of this or that "new
order" believe in their solutions for human ills. Anti-Communism is mere negation. An unshakable position cannot be
founded on a negative. A positive position, I ventured, requires the foundation of a great faith. For Western man that
faith is positive Christianity.

"Christianity is a dead duck," said the writer definitively.
"The number of people with church affiliations is no measure at all. Christianity has been declining as an intense creative force ever since it reached its pinnacle in the thirteenth
century. It is a dead duck," he repeated.

"It persists," commented one of the college instructors, "in
humanitarian ethics. Isn't that enough?"

I did not think it was enough and said so. It is very hard
to be good, I said, and none of us achieves it. Sin is a reality.
One needs an image, an example, a conviction above and be-

yond human morality by which to measure and gauge behavior, including one's own. "I am not good enough to devise
my own ethics," I confessed. "And there will be a great
renascence of Christianity," I predicted.

All the time I was thinking of the *Kirchentag*, the "Day"
of the German Evangelical Church, celebrated in mid-August
in Hamburg while I was in Germany last summer. I have
often doubted whether we reporters correctly assess the importance of events. Certainly neither the world press, nor
the world's intelligence services paid the slightest attention to
the handful of left-wing Socialist émigrés in Switzerland during World War I, led by a Russian who called himself Lenin
and his followers "Bolshevists." Certainly the German General Staff and imperial government who sent him and a few
associates into Russia to stir up trouble for the government
with which they were at war never dreamed that less than a
generation later a Red Army would stand in Berlin.

Only a handful of people originally appreciated the significance of an impoverished unemployed ex-corporal haranguing
beer-hall audiences in Munich, or dreamed that only nineteen
years after he began to assemble crowds most of the world
would be at war against him.

The French writer Anatole France fictionally imagined
the later days of the retired Roman administrator, Pontius
Pilate, who, reminiscing on his rule in Judea, was reminded
of a small sect that was growing up around a personality called
Jesus, whom they claimed had risen from the dead, and whom
Pilate himself had tried. In Anatole France's fictional account, Pilate could no longer recall that minor case, at all.
This is quite probable, I think. And certainly no Roman re-
porter a decade after the Crucifixion would have dreamed
that the very calendar would eventually divide history into
Before and After Christ.

The Evangelical "Day" in Hamburg — the fifth of such assemblies since the war — seemed to me far more significant and important than the meager reports of it in the foreign, or even the German, press. It certainly demonstrated that for tens of thousands of Germans on both sides of the Iron Curtain, the Christian faith is not a "dead duck" but the most positive force of their minds, lives, and souls, the solace of their spiritual wounds, and the steel of their resistance to the brutality of human systems that usurp the role of God.

Much publicized has been the fact that something over a million East Germans came to the interzonal border to receive American food packages distributed by the West German government, but apart from church publications practically no attention was paid to the fact that 20,000 Germans from the Communist area went to Hamburg in mid-August for spiritual comfort and fellowship, after which they hungered more than for bread.

Christians in the German East Zone, as everyone else under Communism, are living dangerously. The churches are open and pastors and priests are performing their ministrations, but the church is relegated to the social periphery and the whole weight of the state is brought to exterminate, especially among youth, every other faith than Marxism. The Press Club of the East Zone of Berlin, which I visited, is dominated by a huge sign: Marxism Is Almighty Because It Is Right. Against the Marxist doctrine of pitiless class struggle to the point of extirpating as subhumans all "class enemies," the pulpits alone preach the doctrine of unity in love through the saving grace of Christ.

One pastor in particular, working in a Red stronghold, conducts Sunday after Sunday a Christian criticism of state evils and state tyranny to the point where his liberty and perhaps his life are seriously endangered. Yet, speaking in Hamburg, he said: "The powers of this world can take no more from a man than his life, and if they take my life, my heavenly Father will give me a new one." He did not speak this pathetically but out of quiet conviction.

In this faith in the immortality of the soul or spirit lies a courageous strength far beyond "humanitarian ethics," for it combines the belief that there is a supernatural or immaterial judge of one's earthly life and that the way one leads this life will influence the next phase of one's existence. It is the difference between living greedily in transitory time and living calmly in eternity.

If Christianity as a living powerful force were dead, encrusted in orthodox dogma and isolated in churchly institutions, it would give no one the strength to overcome the greatest of all human fears — the fear of death. In this very age, modern men have voluntarily risked and accepted death, not as part of an army but as solitary individuals or members of small groups, with the stoicism, even the joy, of the early Christians. I think, first, of the Germans — outstanding among them Helmuth von Moltke — who, during a war involving the future of the German nation, opposed Nazism essentially on Christian grounds, out of Christian devotion and as Christian testimony. Protestants (like Moltke) went to the gallows with Catholics, in a faith that transcended doctrinal differences. Moltke's letters written while awaiting execution are not tragic. They abound in absolute certainty that Christianity will outlast, and eventually triumph over, the forces of hatred and evil.

The Evangelical Christian sees in the forces of skepticism, dissolution, and civil and international war not the end of Christianity but the greatest historical challenge to its eternal truth. The Christian sees his faith as transcending narrow confessional communities, ruling out pharasaical self-righteousness, forbidding the otherworldliness which invites flight into seclusion. Christianity, they think, is of eternity but it is also of this world. It is not only a refuge and a solace. Above all, it imposes a task. Now, of all times, it imposes a task the fulfillment of which is the test of its valid right to existence. It must break through the institutional — as a mission of Jesus Himself was to break through the institutional — to found not merely a church, or churches, but a human society, permeated with Christian idealism as a positive power. The ritual, disciplines, and church fellowship are reminders and strengtheners of the mission, which is not, however, to believers but to unbelievers, and not only to the spirit but to the body, too.

People in Hamburg spoke of the "Christian revolution," the radiation of an impulse to break the calcification of the church, to overcome the seclusion of the minority of "good Christians," and to project the church into the secular world, not as an arm and instrument of the state, but as a healing force. The function of Christianity, to these modern Christians, is not blindly to uphold the status quo in behalf of the Powers That Be, but to be a mission to the poor, the outcast, and the lost; not merely to uphold an otherworldly ideal of justice, but to work for justice on earth; not to found a sect but to further human brotherhood, under the fatherhood of God — and first and foremost by one's own example; not to oppose evil with evil but to overcome it with good; and not to center all Satanic forces under one banner, red or brown, but humbly to realize that there is no person or society that is without sin — "no, not one."

The modern Christian recognizes that as the body without a soul is dead, so the form of a political or social system must be the expression of a vital loving content. The mayor of Hamburg said, relative to the elections that were then in the offing: "Be democratic and Christian. Any people largely and consciously Christian must be, in the nature of their faith, democratic."

But Mayor Brauer was not exhorting his hearers to vote for Mr. Adenauer and the Christian Democratic Union. He himself is a Socialist. In that assembly of 200,000 persons were members of all parties except the extreme right and left, whose world outlook rejects the gospel of reconciliation in the Grace of God. Political partisanship was suspended. Each felt a higher loyalty.

This occurred among a people whose state has been responsible for the greatest catastrophe of modern times; who have been divided by their victors; who have lived through every imaginable political experience.

The Evangelical Christians assembled in Hamburg were conscious of national guilt. But guilt without atonement is only despair, and despair is, itself, guilt. As there is guilt there is also redemption, always the possibility of a new life, in this world as in the hereafter. The tidings are tidings of freedom. Man need not, because he has once done so, forever betray his Lord!

I cannot "prove" that Christianity as a vital, permeating spiritual power, molding social behavior, is a "wave of the future." But to believe that it is doomed because it is ancient, that it cannot break its accumulated incrustations to become again the most radiant force of our culture is equally unprovable. The full Christian revelation has not been made once for all time. Christ was not crucified once and for all. The ever-living Christ dies with every cruel persecution of the innocent, perpetually to be reborn in the hearts of the faithful. Spiritual truth is truth in whatever age, but the tasks of its service change as society changes.

Christian men salvaged what was true, good, and beautiful from even a pagan age, when Western civilization, with the fall of the Roman Empire, collapsed into barbarism. A few centuries later Christianity lifted the spires of cathedrals to the skies, spread institutions of learning from Seville to Warsaw, broke into a miraculous efflorescence of art, added mercy to justice — and betrayed itself in a terrible inter-Christian war. But it never died and it has always been in times of great crisis that new disciples have arisen, sometimes in the most unlikely places, to proclaim again its tidings of great joy.

Perhaps it is nothing that 200,000 men, women, and youths, stood in a drenching rain in the Hamburg city park reciting as in one reverent voice the Lord's Prayer — the great affirmation — pledged to go home, even to an anti-Christian rule, and guard the rekindled flame.

Two hundred thousand persons are not many. But no church could contain their testimony or their mighty hymns as they resounded in public squares. And other uncounted thousands prayed at home with them. Once there were only twelve — and one of them denied, and one betrayed.

It will soon be Christmas 1953. And those whose hearts listen may once again hear the "tidings of great joy," brought now again not to one people, nation, or race, but to all men; not for one day but for all days; not for one time but for all times.

A Foreign Policy for
All Americans*

SOME MONTHS AGO I was asked to discuss American foreign policy with a panel of wives of servicemen, the discussion to be broadcast and televised to the hundreds of stations throughout the world where American women and their children are beside the husbands and fathers who are guarding "the ramparts we watch."

The question that was put by the extremely attractive and responsibly minded service wives as the central theme of the discussion was "What can we women do to help the foreign policy of the United States? And what *is* American foreign policy?"

That is not, indeed, an easy question for anyone to answer. Foreign policy is being made from day to day, by every action taken by the United States that involves nations other than our own. The central aim of every American foreign policy and action is the defense of the best interests of the United States. The Secretary of State, no less than the Secretary of Defense, is part of the defense system. One can precipitate a war, be drawn into one under terribly unfavorable conditions, and even lose a great military victory by false diplomacy.

We live in a world of sovereign states, some of them very old, with ambitions far beyond their own frontiers, or with long established "spheres of interest" brought about by imperial conquests or treaties negotiated with foreign rulers, the

* Written from Dhahran, Saudi Arabia, December 1956.

sudden ending or breaking of which can cause serious disturbances, even catastrophic ones, for all the nations involved.

At the same time new states have arisen in the world, in Asia, Africa, and the Middle East, among peoples who have for centuries been ruled by others. In population, these new states far outnumber all the so-called "Great Powers" of the earth combined. But in power reckoned in terms of organized armies, industrial development and potential, economic organization, and political experience they are inferior to any one of the larger, older, and more "advanced" nations.

But they, too, are sovereign states, and precisely the ones most jealous of their new-found sovereignty.

Generations or centuries of foreign rule, direct or indirect, have left resentments and suspicions that continue even after the rule has ended, and a rejection of the plain fact that the foreign rule has brought great benefits, as well as evils with it. If it were possible to wipe out of any Afro-Asian country everything that Western empires have contributed to establish in them, those countries would be reduced to the most primitive material state, and in some cases to savagery, and this despite the fact that some of them in the far-off past had once had great and flourishing civilizations when Western men were still running around in animal skins, and were themselves the savages.

Furthermore, if everything brought by Western rule were obliterated from memory, even the ideas that have sparked rebellions, raised the demand for independence and self-government, and created the states themselves would be lacking, together with the personalities, experts, and leadership to put such ideas into form. For these are Western ideas, and to an enormous extent the leadership, armies, ministries, bureaucracies, banks, and industrial and agricultural organizers of the new Eastern states are staffed by men who have been educated in British, French, Dutch, and American univer-

sities and colleges, or trained in Western-organized and commanded armies. So that with all the strains, jealousies, mis-
understandings, and even hatreds, there exist mental affinities
which are especially noticeable among the experts of the new
states. To put it simply, however their governments may be
at loggerheads, the Minister of Public Health in any Eastern
country will find an immediate common interest and be eager
to share knowledge and experience with a similar official
from the West — and may even discover that he is invisibly
wearing the same "old school tie."

In a generation as revolutionary as this one, marked by
greater technological, political, and social changes than have
ever converged in any similar span of time, the task of steer-
ing a foreign policy in such a way as to best promote the
security and long-range interests of the United States demands
knowledge, wisdom, foresight, and analytical powers beyond
the capacities of any individual. Even were a man and the
people reporting to him and advising him to be superb historians, and trained anthropologists, sociologists, psychologists, as well as experienced diplomatists, the possibilities of
error in any specific action can hardly be overrated.

All heads and leaders of states, furthermore, operate under
continual pressures of public opinion, which in turn is formed
or influenced by enormous propaganda apparatuses as well as
by objective journalistic reports. Radio alone has enlarged
to an incalculable degree the participation of the public. A
huge proportion of the people of the world are still illiterate.
A generation ago events occurring in the capitals of their
countries were unknown to millions who never saw a newspaper nor could read one if they did. Today even a jungle
savage knows to some degree what is happening in the country where he lives, or elsewhere in the world. He hears of it,
although he cannot read of it. The most illiterate villager in
the poorest mud hut of Egypt could and did follow the

events leading to the Suez crisis. He may have had a highly colored picture of events, but he knew, basically, what had happened. And this adds a new element to the picture. For centuries in much of the world, the common man, or "the masses," had not been reckoned with at all. Affairs of state were conducted by very small coteries of people, many of them pursuing exclusively their personal interests and judging policies entirely by whether they themselves stood to profit or lose by them. No explanations were needed for the vast dumb mass of the people they ruled, whether their rule was native or foreign. Today, no matter what the form of government, and no matter how oligarchical or tyrannical, it operates under universal listening ears.

And all this, even in the most advanced democratic countries, makes the conduct of foreign policy more difficult, and even more dangerous, for errors, or what the people believe to be errors, can bring about popular rebellions and the downfall of governments.

Now, the people, even in so advanced and well-informed a country as the United States, cannot possibly know all the considerations that lead its government to take this or that stand or action in any given situation. None of us, not even those who have spent a lifetime in accumulating knowledge of foreign affairs and trying to analyze it, has continuous access to all the confidential information that pours daily into every foreign office, including our own. We cannot properly weigh alternatives, assessing the results of one possible action against another. We cannot sit in on the intimate conferences between representatives of states, or between the various policy-forming personalities of our own. We cannot be cognizant of all the factors that influence the taking of one action in preference to another, in each specific circumstance, not even with the most alert and competent press. In addition, human prejudice, while it cannot be accurately assessed, cannot be ruled out, and human error is at all times constant. The greatest political leader, the most objective and percipient diplomat, is not God. His judgment, like all human judgments, is fallible.

All this sounds very discouraging, and it *should* discourage all who think that by some nonexistent wisdom and some nonexisting formulas strife, strain, struggle, conflict, danger will somehow resolve themselves and usher in an era of eternal peace and good will among men and nations.

But does it mean that you and I, the service wives and their serving husbands, and all the rest of us who are engaged during most of our waking hours in limited tasks, interests, and hobbies had better give up thinking about American foreign policy?

No, it does not. But we must, I believe, try to think in wider, long-range terms.

First of all, foreign policy cannot be totally divorced from domestic policy. Foreign policy is the face that a nation presents outward to the world. If a country wears one face at home and another abroad, it appears to a world now highly percipient as what it is: double-faced. And it will win no confidence abroad. Nor will it be able in the long run to keep confidence at home and align its own citizens behind its foreign policy.

The United States, from its very birth, has stood for national freedom and the right of self-government.

There has been no slow, centuries-old evolution from this concept. We started with it. We have broadened the base of this concept, as we have broadened the suffrage. But the Declaration of Independence is our original charter of national and personal freedom. And it is at the same time a charter of freedom for all mankind. We did not declare that all Americans were created equal and endowed with certain unalienable rights. We declared that all *men* — all mankind — are so created and endowed.

This sense of an American mission to uphold freedom and equality everywhere, this great liberal doctrine (in the only explicable meaning of the word "liberal") runs through all our patriotic speeches, state papers, national songs, and patriotic poetry. It has perpetually frustrated or restrained all the imperialist jingoists who have arisen in America — as, of course, they have. We simply cannot behave like ourselves — we cannot behave naturally — when we cease to uphold this doctrine. It is the hallmark of America, by which we are recognized, either to be hated or loved.

America has ever been the country of the underdog, of the so-called (and, I think, miscalled) common man. We have welcomed to our shores (not always, certainly, for the noblest reasons) all sorts and conditions of men, and the millions of immigrants who have come have been those who have been most oppressed at home, whether by poverty or social status. No country ever undertook a more hazardous experiment, in faith that not only a state but a cohesive nation could be created out of people from many nations, a large proportion of them, in the eyes of their former nationals, being "the scum of the earth." Yet out of those people, struggling upward in freedom, we have created a nation mighty in power. So another article of the American faith, for which we are known throughout the earth is faith in people. (I know we have not been consistent to this faith at all points. No people are wholly consistent, or ever will be, short of the millennium.) But it is a basic underlying faith. Of all the people in the world we are as a whole the least class-conscious, caste-conscious, or, as a *whole*, race-conscious.

I know that this statement will be disputed in some quarters. There are parts of the world less race-conscious than we, as far as our colored population is concerned. But if we take all three together, and take into account the evolution even in the last-named particular, it is nevertheless true, according to my own experience.

America is both materialistic and generous. I think we are far *too* materialistic, as every reader of my articles in this publication knows. But we wear our materialism with a difference. Americans abhor poverty, not out of materialism alone, but also out of conscience. We just do not believe that suffering imposed by others is good for the soul. The American ideal, shared by rich and poor alike, is that everybody should have a decent standard of living, everybody enjoy leisure, everybody have access to education and recreation. The ideal has influenced the whole capitalist structure of this country, which differs radically from that of many others. Our enterprise is not only "private," it is social. Our businesses are not organized on the basis of the highest possible profit for the lowest possible investment of money and energy, but on the basis of the lowest possible profit per unit of production made possible by the widest possible distribution of goods and services. American business does not see the worker as a coolie to be driven, but as a consumer to be satisfied. For an American wealth is not something to be hoarded but to be spent, and this is both the basis of our giving at home and abroad, and also of our dynamic economy.

Finally, Americans believe in the rule of law — which includes a great many things, such as sanctity of contract. And, let us make no mistake about it, without *some* respect for and means of enforcing contracts there is no civilization, as Mr. Justice Holmes once remarked. Law evolves. It is not only made by legislation and judgments in courts, but by the evolving state of public consciousness and conscience. And it is at all times a power restraining actions in good as well as in evil causes.

America's belief in the United Nations, shared to the same extent by no other Great Power, arises from the conviction that there must be international laws restraining the actions of all states, and limiting their sovereign right to do anything they please.

The Charter of the United Nations prohibits states from going to war except in self-defense. This means that it outlaws *preventive* wars. In so doing, it sets a formidable restriction on the sovereign rights of nations, which throughout history have accepted as part of their sovereignty the right to start a war as well as to repel an aggressor.

An evolving state of consciousness and conscience will, it is to be hoped, result in restrictions of other kinds. The struggle for liberty and self-government does not equate with the right of every rebel movement to commit ghastly crimes — to slaughter women and children in their beds; to organize guerilla bands to plunder, loot, and pillage; to torture and mutilate captives and prisoners. It does not equate with the right to deport whole populations, or render insufferable the lives of foreigners long established in their homes. There will never be a real international law, written or unwritten, until certain basic tenets of civilization itself are revived and universalized. Movements for national liberty and self-government can result in a greatly raised standard of civilization, not only material but more importantly ethical. But they can also result in a return to barbarism. States always carry for generations the brand marks of the means by which they were established. It is better to wait a while for liberty than to defile it by the means through which it is obtained. And equality is bogus unless coupled with equal responsibilities.

But to come to the point and close this discussion: Every American, at home, or wherever he is in the world, and whatever his position, upholds American foreign policy when he thinks and acts in accordance with the American faith.

He is helping to show America's true face to the world when he shows sympathy for the aspirations of all people to national freedom and equality; when he looks down on no one because he is poor, or backward, remembering that a century ago Europeans looked down on us for that reason; when he looks for things to praise rather than blame, and to encourage rather than deplore. He is representing America when his heart, as well as his purse, is generous. He represents America when he finds no sympathy with force or brutality for whatever reason it is employed. He is representing America and furthering the only possibly successful American foreign policy whenever he shows that he believes that power can only be properly used to support such standards of justice and law as already exist and to promote their extension and refinement.

He is representing America and furthering American foreign policy when he thinks and acts patiently, when he is able to digest failures, setbacks, and errors, when he keeps in mind the convulsions shaking this epoch, without losing his faith that in basic matters more things unite than divide mankind; that the love of freedom is universal, as is the desire to lift oneself out of darkness into light, out of ignorance into knowledge, out of squalor into decency, out of sickness into health, out of perpetual danger into security, and out of ever-pending war into peace.

There is no country I have ever visited in the world today, including the one from which I write, where these desires are not manifest at every turn. And those who go with this tide in the affairs of men, whatever the setbacks and frustrations, will not fail — not in the long run.

What Is a World Citizen?

A HIGH SCHOOL student signing herself Mary G—— wrote me some time ago from Maryland:

> Our English class is studying "World Citizens." We would like your opinion on the following questions: What is a world citizen? Who are some world citizens?

Apart from wondering why a class supposed to be studying the structure, composition, and literature of the English language should be studying something else, what shall one answer Mary G?

I am afraid the "world citizen" is like the purple cow. I have never seen one; I hardly hope to see one; and unless further convinced, I'd rather see than be one.

To begin with, what *is* a *citizen?*

The word originates with the word "city," a citizen being an inhabitant of a city, enjoying its freedoms and privileges, as distinguished from a foreigner, or alien not entitled to its franchises. As units of government were extended, a citizen came to be a person owing allegiance to the government of a state and entitled to reciprocal protection from it.

Every citizen in politically advanced countries is not only entitled to its protection of his life, liberty, and lawfully gained property but is also vested with political rights and responsibilities.

The first implication in the word "citizen" is therefore that of domicile, home. Obviously a rolling stone is not a "world citizen." He is a no-citizen, a perpetual alien, a man without a country. When young Garry Davis decided to relinquish his American citizenship to become a world citizen, he very soon found himself a citizen of nowhere.

Citizenship implies relations with a community and with a government. And since there is no world government, no supranational world state, there is no existing possibility of world citizenship. The term merely represents a wish dream, or a myth.

But would it be possible — or desirable?

Those who promote it do so in the interests of world peace. They argue, and logically, that divided warmaking powers in the hands of sovereign states make war an ever-present menace and possibility. But I think they are overoptimistic about the price, even in terms of peace, of achieving a world state, and about the cost and likelihood of its maintenance.

The nearest thing to a world state that ever existed — the Roman Empire — was created by a long-drawn-out series of conquests; maintained itself only by further unremitting military expeditions to suppress rebellions and "enforce peace"; and finally broke up with a crash that plunged its world into darkness and a perpetual devil's brew of bandit wars.

Now, when people talk as glibly as they often do of a world state, it seems to me they fail to face the fact that no world state is at all likely to be created or maintained except by force — the force of one powerful state imposing its will on others. The International Communist Party and the Soviet Union are genuinely bent on creating a world state, but they are logical enough to know that it will not come about through universal voluntary agreement but will have to be imposed, through the subversion of existing social orders and by external force. Certainly no world state could be created before the United States and the Soviet Union fought it out to determine what sort of social and legal order the world state should be. Neither, except in defeat and under dictation, would agree to the premises of the other — and states must be founded on premises. Such a world state would have to be perpetually policed by armies; human freedoms would have to be suppressed and human cultures leveled — for a culture is a mark of differentiation. The plain reality is that the world, in terms of culture, civilization, and consciousness, is *not* "One World." And to try to make it one, against all the realities of life and nature, is far more likely to awake the spirit of rebellion than the spirit of harmony.

What really cements peoples together is not a nation's statutes. These but reflect the civilization, the common way of life, the common conscience. And a person can truly be a citizen of only a country and civilization he has made his own — as much a part of himself as his breathing.

But one cannot make oneself a consciously living part of all the nations and civilizations of mankind. No one can. International Communists, who originally tried to do so — to make themselves part of the mythical "world proletariat" — simply had to discover a substitute motherland, and found it in the Soviet Union.

To be specific and personal, I have the greatest sympathy for India and other oriental countries, and readily acknowledge the greatness of their cultures. Nor do I claim any superiority for the West. For what seem to us to be superiorities are apparently balanced by some subtle law of compensation. But what I do know is that my consciousness is not Indian, or Hindu, or Chinese, and not all the sympathies I may feel will make it so — any more than years of British education could make Mr. Nehru into an Englishman.

I do not want to Americanize other people, nor do I think it possible or desirable. The very fact that I recognize profound differences between the civilizations of the world makes me the opposite of an imperialist, however much imperialism may be dressed up in the garments of uplift and altruism. But neither do I wish my country to be de-Americanized to suit some universal pattern that is bound to be superficial because it can have no roots.

I have resided for years in Europe, full of wonder and admiration for the differentiated achievements of its many nations, and finding innumerable points of contact with most of them. But I never was a citizen, in fact or in spirit, of any country but my own. For I have never been able, for one thing, really to think or to express myself with the best of my mind in any language other than the one I have lived and thought in, and my mental and emotional orientation is American. And this is certainly not unique to me. Almost no writer has ever been able to write with even approximately the same distinction in two languages.

Now it is surely worth noting that the writers and other artists who have attained universal recognition are precisely those who are most deeply rooted and immersed in their *own* culture. There was never a writer more English than Shakespeare, more Italian than Dante, more German than Goethe, more Russian than Dostoevski, or more American than Mark Twain. Yet these are they who have best been able to communicate universally, to all mankind. If anything is great enough, good enough, profound enough, true enough, it reaches up to tower above many nations and many cultures. But, like a tree, the height an artist can attain is in direct proportion to the depth to which his roots go down into native soil. Man, like the universe itself, is limited. And those who nourish themselves on the traditions, aspirations, revelations, and observations of their own peoples are the most robust.

I have observed, also, that an avowed universal love of "humanity" often covers an incapacity really to love anyone or anything with passion and devotion. Sigmund Freud observed this as a symptom of psychoneurosis. It was patently obvious in the case of the traitor Fuchs — the betrayer of atomic secrets to the Russians. The abstract concern with "Humanity" (with a capital H) offers a form of escape. There is always something one can do for one's own family, one's own community, one's own country. But the doing involves coming to grips with real problems and difficulties, and involves real duties and sacrifices. There is precious little anyone can do personally for Humanity at Large, and to transfer one's fidelities to an abstraction is one way of avoiding all obligations to one's fellow human beings.

I write this because it is in the fashion today to decry patriotism as a factor dividing mankind. Nationalism based on an inbred sense of superiority and contempt for others — the aliens, the outsiders — is, indeed, a vicious danger to peace. But patriotism as love of country is actually a feeling shared by all peoples, and though this feeling is directed to various objects, it is a feeling that binds mankind. For only a patriot can understand another patriot, as only a lover can understand lovers. Precisely *because* I love my country I appreciate the love of others for *their* countries. Precisely *because* I regard my country as my primary allegiance I expect others to give their primary allegiances to their countries. I do not have to share their love for and allegiance to their particular object. But I am compelled to respect it, and to await respect in return.

And so, to get back to Mary G's question: I have never known a world citizen, and don't know what it means to be one. But I am quite sure that one is likely to be a beneficent influence in the life of all countries to the extent to which one is a fully conscious and responsible citizen of one's own.

"We Have Nothing to Fear but Fear Itself"

WHEN THE LATE Franklin Delano Roosevelt was elected to the Presidency for the first time, he assumed leadership in a country that was apparently disintegrating from within. Millions were unemployed. Our larger cities were black with breadlines; the smallest communities were bankrupt; banks were about to close their doors; every newspaper carried reports of suicides.

Radicalism was growing in the soil of despair. Thousands of good, respectable people sincerely believed that the American political and economic system was past salvaging — with whatever conceivable reforms — and that Soviet Russia represented "the wave of the future."

Then a warm confident voice said something very great. It said, "We have nothing to fear but fear itself." It seems to me that that simple statement needs repeating today, not only out loud, but by each of us to ourselves. For soberly facing realities there is no present reason for hysteria or despair. Yes, we are in what Arnold Toynbee calls "a time of troubles." Yes, we have made errors — above all errors of ignorance in our leadership. But when have people not lived in times of troubles, and when has any leadership, even the best, been infallible?

I have often been called a pessimist, and the accusation, if accusation it be, is perhaps justified. I have always had a tragic sense of life. I became early acquainted with grief and death. My young mother died when I was seven, and in those

days no one tried to shelter children from the great reality
that all physical life is transient. I have read enough history
to know that no civilization has an eternal lease on life. I am
sufficiently acquainted with scientific thought to know that
this planet itself, and all that it inherits, may sometime dissolve, and without the intervention of man himself in furthering its destruction.

But this sober knowledge is not equivalent to defeatism.
It does not suggest that because we must die, we should commit suicide! On the contrary, it suggests that we should live
while we live, with the greatest possible intensity, finding as
early as possible those interests and pursuits which bring out
the most creative sides of our natures, firm in the knowledge
that, as no one can explain the miracle of organic life, no one,
equally, can disprove what mankind has always believed, that
there is a spiritual existence beyond this existence, for which
man can in some way fit himself.

Similarly the tragic sense of life does not suggest that because civilizations pass, one should hasten their demise; rather
it should make one aware of dangers to be overcome by wise
thought and steadfastness of purpose, and that the precious
goods of civilization should be preserved by each of us.

The most destructive element in the human mind is fear.
Fear creates aggressiveness; aggressiveness engenders hostility;
hostility engenders fear — a disastrous circle.

And what are we wringing our hands about? Do we think
that "modern man is obsolete"? Is it true that man is walking
downward into the abyss? There is no reason to think so.
On the contrary, man has more greatly extended control over
his environment in the last century than in all previous time.
We are not surrounded by people whose faces are defaced
by the pox; we have no reason to anticipate epidemics like
the Black Plague, which destroyed half the population of
Europe five hundred years ago. The life of women, at least

in advanced countries, is no longer expended in bearing four-teen children in the hope that three may survive. We are beginning to defeat the hitherto most baffling internal dis-eases and have already greatly extended the average span of life.

Though the population of the earth has been steadily in-creasing, famine, except in the extremely backward areas, is a thing of the past, for the progress made in agriculture is little short of a miracle. Floods, which once periodically destroyed huge areas, are largely under control.

Although no nation has achieved an economic system of steady expansion, there is no reason to anticipate another such breakdown as occurred in 1929 — which was due to a collapse of private credit — and no reason to believe that other troubles may prove beyond control.

Nowhere in the civilized world today does anyone take poverty for the great masses of the population for granted. Too often we forget that a society in which workmen eat 3000 to 4000 calories of food per day, have their children born in hospitals, live in centrally heated apartments, have access to numerous forms of amusement, dress in a manner almost indistinguishable from the wealthier classes, and take it for granted that most of their children will complete high school is something absolutely new in the history of man-kind!

Throughout most of recorded history "the hewers of wood and drawers of water" were clad in rags, dwelt in filth, worked from dawn to dark, were sustained at bare subsistence, and were weeded out of life by the ruthless operation of the law of the survival of the fittest. To find anything approach-ing such conditions today one must go to the most backward parts of the Orient, and there is no part of the world into which another vision has not penetrated.

"Very well," people say, "civilization *has* advanced, but culture has lagged. Mass education and mass amusement have terribly vulgarized society."

That is true, I think, though I believe that the passions and violences of two great wars have been chiefly responsible for vulgarizing and brutalizing the modern mind. Human progress is alway uneven. Science, rather than art, has attracted the contemporary gifted.

But it is healthy to compare the moving pictures or the dramas of today with those of twenty-five or thirty years ago before one jumps to the nostalgic conclusion that manners and morals have declined. The person of refined tastes can certainly find as much or more in the modern theater and on the screen to inspire and enchant him as he could in, say, 1924. Although, in my belief, modern education has become shallower rather than deeper, the pendulum is swinging. There is more general consciousness of what is wrong and needs improvement than there was a generation ago. And if this postwar epoch is bad, the youth today compare favorably with those of the former postwar era of bathtub gin and the "lost generation."

"Yes," the defeatist continues, "but look at the spread of Communism, that destroyer of all civilized social orders."

Let us, indeed, look at it.

The Bolshevik revolution, at the close of World War I, was hailed as a great liberation movement by many of the finest spirits in Western society. In the most advanced countries, liberal hearts and minds kindled to it and supported it and the premises on which it was based. Among the early pro-Communists were leading poets, philosophers, and men of letters.

What is the history of these early, distinguished pro-Communists, such as André Gide, John Dos Passos, Edmund Wilson, Ignazio Silone, and Arthur Koestler? It is a history of disillusionment. If Communism can extend itself only in the most backward countries, by ruse (the seizing of power by armed guerrilla movements in war) or by open armed attack, and if its promoters today are either half-baked idealists or cynical professional masters of the *coup d'état*, is that not in itself a considerable reason for confidence?

And this disillusionment is not only the death of another bright hope, which, of itself, would be discouraging.

The fact is that while Communism has been demonstrating its incapacity to create anything but a ruthless slave state of servile robots, and has to defend itself even before the Russian people by beating out, day and night, the theme that Russia is surrounded by "capitalist, cannibalistic war-mongers," capitalism as Karl Marx described it has practically ceased to exist in all advanced countries, and its evolution has confounded all his predictions.

It is imprecise to say that the world outside the Soviet Union lives in a "capitalist" society — i.e., one in which the owners of capital dominate and control the state and society. Western civilization lives in a cooperative technological society, partly private capitalist; partly socialistic, in which policies are made by the interplay of many minds, needs, and organized associations, including those of capital, labor, and farmers.

In practical terms Henry Ford was more of a revolutionist than Marx. Ford saw that poverty was incompatible with successful technological enterprise, that interest charges were a more parasitic burden on enterprise than profits, and that profits themselves could more securely be maintained by very small returns per unit of vast production and turnover.

Last year a cash-and-carry chain enterprise that sells meat and groceries at relatively low prices did a three-billion-dollar business at a profit on sales of a fraction over 1 per cent. If this profit is regarded as a service charge, it means that for every $100 spent by the housewife she got $98.60 worth at actual cost!

If Communism means the fullest use of the national capital, the widest distribution of the national product, and the abolition of a proletarian status — and if it doesn't mean that what *does* it mean? — then the United States can claim to be the most advanced Communist country in the world!

And it is also the most cooperative and community-conscious. In no other country are so many individuals voluntarily organized into associations to care for the needy, support and serve in hospitals, clean up municipalities, improve schools, expose corruption, beautify villages, inform voters on issues, improve race relations — hundreds of thousands of persons pooling their energies and contributing from their pockets for purposes which promise them no personal gain whatever.

"What is it all worth," say the defeatists finally, "since we are heading straight into another Great War?"

Are they so sure of that?

There will not be another Great War unless the Soviet Union decides directly or through satellites to attack certain areas vital to Western security, or unless this country loses its head. The United States and the nations associating themselves with us have renounced aggression against each other and against anyone else. We are purely a defense association. The Soviet Union may not believe this to be true; perhaps we do not do all we could to make it clear to everyone on earth that it is true. Nor is it, I think, a good idea to let the Soviet Union think that in a crisis we might back down.

But if the Soviets are convinced that they are taking overwhelming risks, will they actually launch an attack which would result in hurling the entire American industrial armament at Soviet centers?

I somehow don't think they will. They will certainly go on trying to keep us running around the world, resisting non-Russian armies here or there. They will go on trying to destroy the value of the dollar and bankrupt the American economy by political and economic measures. We shall have to be wiser and more prudent, I think, than we have been in the past five years. But I am sure it is an error to believe that everything is working well in the Soviet world. The Soviets are not likely to forget that Soviet armies alone mutinied in the last war, and a condition of anarchy induced by war is not one with which highly centralized despotisms, ruling disillusioned peoples, can most successfully cope. From the Soviet viewpoint I can see many reasons for caution, and I assume Soviet leaders see them, too, no matter how loudly they bark.

If many of our allies are weak and disillusioned, wouldn't it be better to cheer them up by keeping steady rather than adding American disillusion and defeatism to theirs?

And if the worst should come to the worst, and we should have only ourselves, isn't "ourselves" a very, very great thing to have? Does anyone really doubt that all lances would break on a continentally united people who fiercely love their land and who can, if they ever had to, live on their own resources and ingenuity?

If I thus push the possibilities to the ultimate, it is only because I believe that courageous facing of such possibilities is a first step toward overcoming fear. The greatest human enemy is fear — a greater enemy than the Soviet Union, the Soviet's greatest ally, and the psychological force most likely to drive us into the impetuosity which could bring on a Great War.

Great nations are only defeated when they are defeated in their own minds, and every sign of fear is a psychological battle won against us.

Truly "We have nothing to fear but fear itself."

On Loyalty

WE LIVE IN strange and troubled times of which one manifestation is the concern of public and private functionaries with the question of "Loyalty." Debates rage over the question to what extent "loyalty oaths" should be demanded of public employees, teachers, and college professors. Against such oaths some citizens invoke freedom of speech and conscience, while others demand the opportunity to purge "subversive" or possibly subversive persons from the public payrolls.

But exactly what "loyalty" is, and how "subversive" may be interpreted, remains unsatisfactory in definition.

I have always doubted whether anyone changes his mind or character by taking a formal official "oath." Certainly Communists don't. Indeed, the mechanism of the International Communist Party would be unable to function unless its key figures were quite willing to swear — for instance to immigration authorities — that they were not, and never had been, Communists.

But beyond this, the loyalty oaths of today are largely negative. They ask our citizens to record what they are against rather than what they are for.

Then, there creeps into the picture the concept of "hundred per cent Americanism," and the idea of "divided loyalties" that may include other nations than one's own. Yet at the same time the United States is a member of the United Nations, which demands, let us say, a certain extension of the spirit of loyalty. There is always, also, the question of what one owes to the state, what one owes to one's national society, what one owes to creeds and institutions not defined by state lines, such as religion, and what one, as a person, owes to his own conscience and to himself.

If we think carefully about it, this question of loyalty becomes very complicated indeed, involving a whole philosophy of life.

Loyalty, or fidelity, are basic ingredients of human character, and an individual without them is not a person at all. Every social institution, from the basic unit of the family to the most august instruments of state power is based on the assumption of loyalty, and maintained by the reality of it. The words "treachery," "treason," "traitor," are as ugly as any in the language, and under certain conditions carry the highest legal penalties, and rightly so. For to "betray" is surely as loathsome as to kill, and may, in fact, destroy far more human lives than the worst murderer.

Loyalty to one's country is, in essence, loyalty to one's family, one's community, and one's self, and, to my mind, all international loyalties must be based upon this primary premise. One can have many friends, but one has only one father and mother. One can be attracted to many men or women, but one has only one wife or husband (in most of the world), at least at one time. One can, in a platonic sense at least, love all children. But natural law and one's primary obligation is to love and care for one's own.

And, as I doubt the filial capacities of anyone who does not, or is unable, to love his own parents, or the very capacity to love at all in a person who can be faithful to no spouse, or the existence of paternal or maternal instinct in those who claim to love all children but are indifferent to their own, so I doubt the value of anyone to an international society who is not to begin with a patriot of his own country.

For we cannot even begin to understand other peoples, unless we understand that all of them, with very few exceptions, love their countries as you and I love ours.

On this rock, sooner or later, International Communism, led by uprooted anti-patriots, will surely founder.

Patriotism is a form of love, and all love involves the desire to serve. The concept "patriot" cannot be defined merely as a person who is obedient to the state, and keeps its laws, nor does it involve conformity to whatever the dominant opinion of the times may be. Patriotism and loyalty are *active* and *eager* forces. Being rooted in love, they involve responsibility more than "rights"; and they often produce rebels, though they never produce traitors. For the rebel acts out of *love;* the traitor acts out of hate or frustration.

The American rebel-revolutionaries, to take an illustration, were traitors to no one. The British government of the time did not see it that way, though some Britons did — notably Edmund Burke. The Colonists rebelled, to be sure, against a state power. But they did not seek to overthrow the government of Great Britain. If Englishmen were satisfied with George III, and what was, at that time, a semifeudal caste society, that was their own business. It did not suit the Colonists (largely English) of a new country, with ideas of their own, and a (very English) desire for self-government.

The difference between rebellion and treason is so profound that it is recognized even by one's enemies. Because the Americans (like most of the Irish) were rebels, but not traitors, they were able, once the rebellion was successful, speedily to compose their differences with Great Britain and establish relations of mutual honor and respect more enduring than we have had with any other nation.

Similarly one can rebel against one's own government, out of love for the society which one feels the government to be misrepresenting or encroaching upon. Rebellion becomes treason, however, when the gates are opened to those who do not share the patriotism that can instigate rebellion — who *cannot* share it, because their hearts and loyalties are elsewhere. To invite foreign control is treason, for the very simple reason that no one is ever able truly to serve a society of which he is not himself a member, and to which he feels no primary obligation.

The people of the South, in the great American tragedy of the Civil War, were rebels but not traitors. Even though they sought to dissolve the American Union, its prime upholder and their greatest opponent, Abraham Lincoln, who believed their rebellion deadly wrong and whose judgment has been justified by history, never charged their rebellion as treason. The War Between the States was a strictly family affair over differences of constitutional interpretation and between two regional ways of life. But General Robert E. Lee was as much a patriot as Ulysses S. Grant. Had he, however — which is unthinkable — invited in the armies of a foreign power to subdue the North at the cost of the subservience of both North and South, there would have been no generous gesture at Appomattox, no memorial at Arlington, and indeed, there would be no America. But as long as one American, northern or southern, lived in whom was even the faintest historical remembrance, in whom resided the dimmest spark of loyalty and honor, in whose heart the most primitive love of country budded, if it never bloomed, and as long as the memory of the old martyrs had not faded utterly away, his name would be execrated, however silently. And if ever the turn of history presented the opportunity, rebellion would answer treason, and the state would be overthrown, violently perhaps, brutally perhaps — but by lovers and patriots.

And every patriot in the world, though he had never set foot in America, would rejoice.

Loyalty is not a formal thing. It involves honor, conviction, faith, belief. It involves everything one lives by; everything one loves.

As an American, I gratefully realize that I am heir to a great material inheritance. Nature itself endowed this land as few nations have ever been blessed. Rich in its soil, timber, and mineral resources; superb in the beauty of its landscape and the variety of its climate; built by hard-working and God-fearing forebears, in sweat, blood, tears, and laughter — and by self-seeking buccaneers, too; gifted with ingenuity; hospitable by nature; protected by oceanic distance but careless of space and time — to you, who came and went before me, and honestly earned your way, I pledge my loyalty. Like you, I will try to earn my way.

As an American, I recognize that I am heir to a revolutionary tradition that distrusts all concentrations of power, whether in oligarchies of blood, wealth, or other massed economic pressure; or whether in the hands of an overweening state. I swear I shall remain loyal to that revolutionary tradition, against all counterrevolutions whatsoever, even when they deceitfully call themselves "New Orders."

As an American, I am endowed with civil rights which demand reciprocal obligations; rights which must daily be justified and earned, and protected against all, who in their very name would seeek to take them away.

I swear I will do my best to protect those rights by the fulfillment of my obligations.

As an American, I will work at the height of the energy and efficiency I possess, knowing that a country and community prosper and move forward only on that surplus of energy which is not immediately consumed.

As an American, in a society striving for freedom and equality of opportunity, I will demand of no fellow man or woman more than I am, myself, willing to give in exchange, and taking account of differences in natural endowment of energy. I will strive with all my power to do as I would be done by, in every human relation, whether as employer or as employed, whether as neighbor or as citizen, realizing that democracy is an organic fellowship and not a mere formal and legal organization.

As an American, I will hold no fellow American in disrepute because of his race, religion, or national origin, judging as I would be judged, respecting every social and political opinion that springs from love of this country and community, however much I may disagree with them. But as a self-respecting person I will demand as much for my own opinions, for none can respect others who do not respect themselves. And I will set my face intransigently against treason, knowing that no one who is false to his own can be loyal to anything.

As an American, I will be candid in my public life, opinions, and affiliations, willing to answer for them to all who enquire, and recognizing that there is no constitutional guarantee that non-conformity must be rewarded by popularity, and that freedom, like everything else worth having, entails risk.

As an American, I shall recognize majority rule, but attribute to it no monopoly on wisdom, truth, or righteousness. I shall not enquire how many people hold an opinion, but whether or not it be justified in reason, truth, and experience.

As an American, I shall recognize that every human society that has ever existed and flourished at a high level has demanded a degree of obedience and authority; of sanctity of contract; of security of the human person; of the safeguarding of private property; of the regulation of relations between the sexes; and of the satisfaction of those basic needs essential to the maintenance of life. All liberty is therefore limited by the necessities of culture; all culture by the necessity of liberty; and all else is savagery and barbarity.

As an American, I shall sympathize with and support all peoples striving in their own patriotism after what Americans, as members of an organized community, demand for themselves. But I shall also demand reciprocal respect for Americans.

As an American, I have unswerving faith in the triumphant survival of societies of free and cooperative human beings, and in the energizing strength of creative love over destructive hate — whether between persons, groups, classes, or nations. No matter how dark the way, how great the errors, how discouraging the setbacks, how painful the sacrifices, I shall never abandon this faith. It is justified by wayward history. It is promised by my religion, and by the insight of all religions that have ever swayed the minds and hearts of numerous bodies of men.

I believe in God.

This is my loyalty oath.

Concerning Tolerance

THE OPEN MIND has been greatly praised, but somebody once said that an open mind was often a mind with nothing in it. It has also been said that "to understand all is to forgive all," but it is perhaps truer to say that to understand nothing is to forgive everything.

Every saw and every truism needs inspection. Words need periodic inspection. And one word that needs some reconsideration is the great word "tolerance." For it has been abused past recognition. From being a positive expression of respect for other people's rights, it has become a weasel word for the avoidance of responsibility.

The Latin root of the word "tolerance" refers to things that can be borne, endured, are supportable. The intrinsic meaning of "tolerance" is the capacity to sustain and endure, as of hardship. From this comes the inferential meaning of patience with the opinions and practices of those who differ. It is interesting that the word is used in connection with the coining of money and with machinery, to indicate the margin within which coins may deviate from the fixed standard, or the dimensions or parts of a machine from the norm.

But the word "tolerance" does not suggest that everything is supportable and that any amount of deviation is allowable. It suggests that one's principles and standards should be tempered with patience, and with readiness to subject them to modification, through practical or intellectual tests. But it does not suggest that one should have no principles or standards. In the contemporary world, I find that for many people this is, however, exactly what they mean by tolerance: a vapid openness to the condoning of anything. Tolerance carried to this conclusion is anarchy. It is not an instrument of civilization, but an instrument of barbarism.

We are not tolerant of diphtheria bacilli, tuberculosis germs, or cancer cells. We do not assert their right also to live and work. We know that they cannot continue to exist if the organism which they have entered, or in which they have grown, is also to continue to exist. Therefore we eradicate them with the greatest intolerance. We know that there is no way for noncancerous tissue to come to an agreement with cancerous tissue. There is no possible *modus vivendi* between them. Therefore, a cancer is eradicated.

But in our social and political life we seem to think that democracy is only a casual host for the entertainment of all conceivable viewpoints and organizations, including those whose clear intention it is to destroy the host. Instead of allowing that margin, even a very wide margin, for variation which is the essence of tolerance, we entertain those in whom there is no speck of tolerance whatsoever for democracy itself, or for tolerance itself, and who seek to substitute for ordered popular government under law a regime of dictatorship and violence.

The margin of tolerance in a democracy, or in any other organized and civilized state ruled by law, stops when standards essential to the continuance of an orderly and civilized community are seriously menaced. It is impossible, for instance, to continue any sort of orderly, civilized, and legal community at all if the police powers are captured, by whatever legal methods, by gangsters, and then used to destroy the law, the courts, private property, all civilian immunities, and to kill people arbitrarily, without indictment or trial.

It is of not the slightest consequence, for instance, that the American Communist Party is a legal organization, that it pays lip service to democracy — and, indeed, calls itself democracy's agent — and that it does not seek to make its way by throwing bombs or by other acts of violence, but uses instead the legal methods of persuasion and organization, assisted by more dubious instruments of slander and intimidation. Its object is what is important, and its object is to destroy the law, and to substitute for law the absolute dictatorship of a party itself dictatorially ruled, and acting as the self-appointed agents of what they choose to delineate as the proletariat, or "working masses." This is demonstrably the object of the Communist Party. This is the actual form of organization that exists in Soviet Russia, and it is a form of organization that has been consistently praised and never denounced by any Communist Party leader — or by any one of them who has continued thereafter to hold his position. The American Communist Party is in alliance with the Communist Party of Russia. And, therefore, the American Communist Party is outside the bounds of possible tolerance by anyone who is not a Communist, for the achievement of its object is incompatible with the continuance of our existence as a civilized community ruled by law.

Exactly the same thing holds true for the German-American Bund and its kindred and supporting organizations. The legality of their methods does not obscure the fact that their object is to destroy the essential integrity of this country both as an independent power and as an organized commonwealth. If anyone doubts that, after what has happened in Central Europe, he is verging on feeble-mindedness. Their program is to deprive millions of our citizens of their citizenship rights and make them "subjects" of the rest of us. The pattern of society which is their model is the dictatorship of a gang, knowing no limitations of ethics or law, and ruling with total arbitrariness. As I write these lines, this regime, if you can call it a regime, is engaged on an international plunder expedition.

It is impossible to tolerate the absolutely incompatible. Toleration then leads either to the destruction of order and civilization by capitulation, or to civil war. It cannot possibly lead anywhere else. You cannot make a "pact" with Communism or Nazism. They demand all or nothing; that is their nature. Therefore there is, in respect of them, no supportable plea for the rights of civil liberty. Al Capone could not appeal to civil liberties for the right openly to organize his gang, with the protection of the police. No state can tolerate that which is hostile to the very concept of the state as such.

In this country we can tolerate every political group, from the right to the left, Socialists and Bourbons, provided they are not acting as agents of foreign powers and do not have as their object the substitution of the legally ordered society by the rule of violence. To extend tolerance to such is to abdicate intelligence and prepare for the extermination of tolerance itself.

We Can Conquer Minds and Hearts

ON A PLANE between Rome and Cairo a Norwegian passenger lent me a week-old American magazine to read. It contained a sensational preview of what, it was predicted, would be the next great American scientific achievement. Most of the magazine issue was devoted to this prediction, under the title, "We Can Conquer Space." Numerous scientists contributed, and all of them agreed that given the money for continued research and experimentation, the United States might very soon realize another conquest, surpassing that of disintegrating the atom.

What was proposed and declared to be possible and even imminent was the creation of a ship or "station" that, rocketed into planetary space outside the orbit within which moves the earth, would be an artificial satellite, a tiny man-made star as it were, completely detached from the planet on which we live and from all its physical laws. Out there, in space, there would be no gravity, no weight, and no air. In fact, said the authors, the environment of such a "space station" could be described only as "nothingness." Yet this station in nothingness would be occupied by a human crew, who, dressed in an armor (depicted in illustrations) to make them resemble mechanical robots rather than men, would carry with them their own air, re-create within their narrow room shot into space their own weight — to enable them, for instance, to get food into their mouths — and manage to re-create on the most primitive plane the conditions essential to the survival of human life in a sphere where there is no organic life, human or otherwise. The greatest hazard, the authors averred, would be from meteors or meteor-dust, but they assured the reader that invention and ingenuity would also find defenses against these; the greatest morale disturber would be boredom — the awful boredom of existence in nothingness.

But why should man seek to enter "nothingness," a sphere where by definition there is nothing whatever to discover and gain for the human race, unless, perhaps, one might learn a little more than is now known about the structure of the universe? But that was not the projected object of such a "conquest." The object was not to add to knowledge; this is not the project of astronomers. Astronomers are to be but its handmaidens. The object in artificially and mechanically creating a position outside the earth and its laws, and a point from which all this planet, as it pursues its course of movement would be vulnerable at every point, is to achieve the final perfection of war.

For years writers of scientific fiction have imagined the invasion of the earth from other planets by other beings than we, creatures (if "creatures" exist elsewhere) who are not "Man." Some years ago the actor Orson Welles, reading on the radio a dramatization of the late H. G. Wells's *War of the Worlds*, sent part of our population into panic as they were led to imagine that an invasion from another planet had actually begun.

The authors of the article did not take that danger seriously at all. Their space station is not designed for defense against the aggressions of another world. The invasion of this planet which the scientists dream as possible is to be by its own inhabitants, able from a contrived station in stellar space to bombard it with atomic destruction and so become its masters in war. Thus, from nothingness this only somethingness we know could be invaded, not by men as men (dropping from parachutes, for instance), but by their destructive engines; and thus, this planet could be made to lie as one single turning target, vulnerable from a point in interstellar space.

A caption in the article inquired, "What Are We Waiting For"! It instructed the readers that all that is necessary to achieve this possibility of world mastery is four billion dollars — of the taxpayers' money, of course: of your money, and mine.

It seems to me that one thing we should wait for, and wait a long time, is for thought.

Since I handed back the magazine to my Norwegian fellow passenger, I have been continuously haunted by the article. I do not know enough of physics, engineering, or astronomy to form a judgment of whether the proposals for the conquest of space are soundly based, scientifically, or likely to be realized in foreseeable time. But is there not an element of what normally would be called criminal insanity in some of modern scientific genius? Is it necessary to do everything that a few men conceive it possible to do, regardless of the results?

The world — or rather *our* world, on this planet — has just celebrated the five-hundredth anniversary of the birth of Leonardo da Vinci, probably the greatest universal genius mankind has yet produced. We know him best as the artist who painted the Mona Lisa, the lady of the cryptic, haunting smile.

But Leonardo was also a scientist and inventor, who five centuries ago designed a submarine. He never perfected it, because as he noted in writing, he feared it might be used as "an instrument of assassination." He did not think that the moral nature of man had developed to the point where he could be entrusted with such a treacherous and ingenious machine.

Who was the greater and wiser man? Leonardo, who put restraints upon his own scientific genius, or some modern scientists who seem to think themselves above and not responsible to the human race?

I thought of that four billion dollars — as a mere beginning, of course — as I continued my travels in territories destroyed by the last war, in Europe, North Africa, and the Middle East, seeing daily before my eyes the skeletons of once fair cities, which generations of engineers, architects, artists, gardeners, and laborers had created as homes for man. And I saw them building anew; docks and quays for the ships of peaceful commerce; factories for the manufacture of necessary and useful things; schools, homes, temples, and churches.

As the plane in which I was traveling sped over the Libyan Desert, the pilot called our attention to the fact that below us lay El Alamein, scene of one of the most desperate battles of the last war. Nothing was there to recall it, only wastes of barren sand. But from a newspaper put on the plane at Tripoli, I learned that Englishmen and Germans were cooperating in a joint expedition to search for, uncover, and reinter in cemeteries the bleached bones of their youthful dead.

I visited new countries, carved by the victors out of old empires, and talked with their officials about their problems — countries where not one person in a thousand can read or write; where flies still eat at children's eyes inducing blindness; where diseases that science can prevent or cure — malaria, tuberculosis, and endemic worm diseases caused by parasites in stagnant waters — reduce human energy to a dragging existence, if they do not cause death.

I talked with physicians in new social centers — "We have 150 now; we need fifteen hundred" — and the story was nearly always the same: "We don't get at the *root* of the trouble. The patients we cure come in a month later with the same diseases. If only all the waters could be simultaneously treated with copper sulphate we would stop the life cycle of the animals on whom the parasites breed. But there is never enough money."

Four thousand million dollars — to conquer nothingness. For that money populous states could be irrigated and deserts made to blossom. Four billion dollars is nearly five times the totatl budget of one Middle Eastern state; a budget which must cover war reconstruction, education, sanitation, hospitals, irrigation, roads, and all costs of administration.

And along the way I paused to contemplate the ruins of once great civilizations; to observe that nearly 3000 years before Christ, men performed extraordinary engineering feats, built great buildings of hand-cut stone, carved exquisite vessels and remarkable sculptures of alabaster and porphery; spun fine linen, made cosmetics; and built great dams and sluices for water. I talked with world-famous archeologists, asking, "Why did all this perish?" And usually the answer was, "The men who did all this overexpended their energies in war."

And wherever I went, in Europe and the Middle East, I

read and heard anxiety expressed about America. On the morning that I wrote this article, the Egyptian newspaper *Al Mukattam* summarized these anxieties and complaints:

> *America no longer seems to look at the world from the humanitarian viewpoint, but only from the viewpoint of military bases and strategy. For this reason America is failing to win our friendship, in spite of all her efforts and good intentions. The Americans we came to know before the last war were men of education, industry, and philanthropy who were concerned about our lives and progress and thus gained our friendship. This is what we want now.*

We are thus set to conquer the bleak nothingness of space while the somethingness of our own human world calls to us in frustration and pain. And in the very birthplaces of human civilization the ruins of past ages cry a warning. There, on the Mediterranean North African coast, broken columns and the conformations of dusty rubble remind one that a great city-state, with temples and stadiums, baths, theaters, and gardens, once rose white and gleaming above the sea. And broken pieces of sculpture reveal bodies and faces so like our own as to be startling: fair faces, full of energy, will, intelligence. No people like them live today in the "backward area" where this great and prosperous city once stood, but dark and ragged Bedouins, herding their poor flocks of sheep and goats and dwelling in tents and caves.

What happened here to bring such beauty low? Not external war, but two internal revolts from which the city never recovered. And as I looked upon the ruins I remembered that strange prophecy that Sunday School children repeat without much thought:

> *Blessed are the meek, for they shall inherit the earth.*

The meek of this world — the poor, the downtrodden, the backward, the ignorant — they are no target for the conquerors of space, who may one day launch their billion-dollar weapons from some artificial Mars.

When the cities are gone there may be left the deserts and the mountains, the tent and cave dwellers, the herdsmen and the peasants, and the savages of the jungles, from whom the upward climb of civilization may again, someday, begin.

But may we not rather hope and believe that instead of conquering space, the sphere of nothingness from which to bombard this planet, we may yet turn from such nihilism and bend our energies to conquer the evil in ourselves and the sickness of this planet — this one small sphere in the universe which alone, among the myriad stars has been given to the race of Man? Must we continue to collaborate to write his epitaph?

Only the Rose

THE JOINT RESOLUTION introduced into Congress by Senator Margaret Chase Smith of Maine and Representative Frances Bolton of Ohio to make the rose the national American flower stirred up quite a ruckus. It was surprising to learn that there are people who don't like roses. I never believed that anyone could be inimical to the rose unless he suffered from rose fever. But, no, there are rosephobes, and (among them gardeners) those who say that roses (meaning, of course, those beautiful hybrids with tags on them) are hard to grow, require care out of all proportion to the results, are thorny, and susceptible to any number of blights, and aphids too.

National and international issues entered the discussion. Anglophiles said we are stealing the English national flower. Anglophobes said that as usual we were aping the English, and remembered George the Third.

Others asked belligerently *what* rose, saying there are roses and roses, and if the rose is to become an American national emblem, let it be a native *American* rose and not one of those aliens.

But even that would not settle the matter, for there are three specifically American native roses. The "Pasture Rose" grows wild from Newfoundland west to Wisconsin and south to Georgia; the "Prairie Rose," a wild climber, clambers over old walls from Ontario to Florida and Texas; the "Cherokee Rose" (Georgia's state flower), vigorous, evergreen, and also a climber, romps through the South, acting as though it were born there. But it wasn't; it's not a *Mayflower* descendant among roses. Though it was here long before the first Pilgrims, its origins were in Japan and China. How it got here nobody knows, not even the rose.

There I went making all-unconsciously, a rhyme:

> *Nobody knows,*
> *Not even the Rose.*

May not the prestige of the rose, among English-speaking people, be largely due to the poets who have celebrated the rose because it makes their homework easier? Few words are so easy to rhyme as "rose." In rows it grows, in wind it blows, in dusk it glows, while the cow lows, the peasant mows, and anything goes with rose. The daisy is a pretty flower and a pretty word — many a lass has been named Daisy (or Violet, or Rose). But it's hard to rhyme Daisy with anything but lazy and crazy.

Iowa's state flower is the "Wild Rose" — any one of them; North Dakota's the "Prairie Rose"; and New York's is the Rose — native, cultivated, or hybrid is not defined. The District of Columbia chose the American Beauty Rose (which looks to me like flag-waving before foreign embassies, and an expression of economic superiority — for the American Beauty is pre-eminently a hothouse growth, retailing when I last inquired, at $12 a dozen).

By choice of the states, the violet — "by a mossy stone, half hidden from the eye" — is a runner-up with the rose, having been chosen by Illinois, New Jersey, Wisconsin, and Rhode Island. Most of the state choices are wild flowers. Alabama, with fine disregard for hay fever, has the goldenrod; Arizona, with pioneer determination to make an asset from its desert peculiarities, chose the giant cactus (nice for the dining room table). Rose-loving Senator Smith's own state of Maine chose the pine cone — if that's a flower! Vermont, which has more cows than people, apparently let the cows choose — Red Clover.

I take my hat off to rugged Wyoming. Its state flower is Indian paintbrush. A pretty flaming thing it is, if you can forget what it does to your hayfields and cattle. Its beauties are completely lost on me. Away with it! Never brighten my door again!

This controversy reveals, however, what extremely strong feelings people have about flowers, even when their tastes are, in general, catholic and tolerant, like mine. An energetic group has been sponsoring the gladiolus as the national flower. Now, although I think the gladiolus is all right in its place, its place in my garden is strictly limited and I think it has already usurped the national scene far beyond its due. It's the national flower of hotel rooms, lecture platforms — and funerals. Handsome it certainly is, like a "well-groomed" woman; not a hair out of place, and not a bit of charm. Stiff and scentless, who could possibly choose the gladiolus above — oh, almost *any* other flower!

Put it down to prejudice. Admitted. I am prejudiced against dahlias. Not *seriously* — I don't want to deprive them of their vote, or send them back where they came from. I know perfectly nice people and good patriotic Americans who *adore* dahlias. But they leave me stone cold, and I can't possibly explain why, any more than a woman can explain why she is instantly attracted to one man, and not at all to another.

I'm no soul mate of the dahlia.

Affinities to flowers are, I think, intensely personal, like affinities to colors and scents. I have friends who won't have a delphinium in their gardens because they don't like blue flowers, whose color vanishes with sundown. But I rather especially love blue flowers. No blues, to my mind, outside the stained glass of Chartres or the waters of the river Rhone, are so magical as the multitoned blues of delphinium.

Theirs are not the only blues. In May, at our Vermont home, the ground under a small plum orchard is blue-carpeted with wild violets, hundreds of thousands of them — a little miracle. The wild Siberian iris, the "Blue Flag," shines in swamps like swatches of fallen sky. It is celebrated in Edna St. Vincent Millay's beautiful poem, "The Blue Flower in the Bog." Later, in the annual garden the Chinese forget-me-not is as limpidly blue as the eyes of a blue-eyed child. Only the perennial flax is as purely blue, and transparent as the sky. The intense, darker blue of bachelor's buttons sings like a note of music; the blue morning glory clambering up a trellis at a kitchen door is lovelier to me than wisteria, and, in the herb garden, are the lilac-blue thistles of chives.

I am inclined to think that the flowers we most love are those we knew when we were very young, when our senses were most acute to color and to smell, and our natures most lyrical. We love flowers because of associations, long forgotten and unconscious associations of time, circumstance, and place — above all of place.

I was a northern child, accustomed to the comings and goings of seasons; a country child, who roamed the woods, to come when winter was hardly over and there was still snow against the north side of the house, upon a pool of pure gold — the marsh marigold, surrounded by a thicket of pussy-willows — or upon a bank snow-white or blood-red with trillium. We sought the frail hepatica, the arbutus and the bloodroot, for the woven paper baskets that we hung on neighbors' doorknobs to announce the first of May. These wild northern flowers to me are spring, the season of childhood and youth, the time when one is in love with everything. And the memory when one is no longer young, and no longer in love with everything.

Summer in the farther north begins with the lilac, the flower of late May and earliest June, which throws out its powerful scent in competition with the last apple blossoms.

When I was a child the lilacs sang to me "School will soon be out, school will soon be out" — and so it is today. Summer is at the door — lovely, lovely summer, when school is out and I can live again in the country, the only place really to live.

I would choose the lilac over the rose — the common lilac, with its glossy heart-shaped leaves and scented candelabra of bloom; the lilac that flourishes in any soil, renews itself from the roots, survives the iciest winters, and blossoms beside old cellar holes, outliving buildings and tenants alike — if *I* were to decide the national flower. And what Northerner would not celebrate the lilac's distant cousin, the citrus-scented syringa?

But suppose I had been a child in Mississippi, Alabama, Georgia, or Southern California? Could the lilac, then, possibly mean what it does to a Northerner? Would not my earliest, most lyrical associations have been with the magnolia, the bougainvillaea, and the camellia? I admire them greatly, but with the detached admiration of a visitor to the botanical gardens. They evoke nothing. No tears come to my eyes, no memories crowd my mind and heart. They do not recall *my* papa and mama.

My papa and mama are associated with lilac and "golden glow." With the white, coral, cerise, and particolored phlox, all in a bevy, like little girls in party dresses. With the shy lilies-of-the-valley; the fair narcissus; the peony (called by the Germans the Corpus Christi Rose — rose of the body of Christ), and all the scents of these. Childhood memories are with the fragile stars of cosmos; the clove-scented stocks; the many-colored snapdragons, whose mouths childish fingers made to roar. They are with "pincushion flowers," which bear the horrid name "scabiosa," and the myriad-colored trumpets of salpiglossis. They are with the acrid scents — which some find odorous — of calendula and marigold and chrysanthemum. They are with the modest, greeny, deliciously aromatic spires of mignonette, the heavy, heady scent of mountain heliotrope, the sweet lavender, which, dried and in cheesecloth bags, scented my mother's linen closets.

My garden is my recaptured childhood, seeing in memory my father training sweet peas on brush. "It is a cool flower, plant it low and early." My garden is everything that ever happened to me of any permanence. "Far and forgotten as a scene in cameo," the gray-eyed man, raking the seed bed for his frail darlings of sun and rain, the man who loved Jesus, flowers, and English poetry. I love what my father loved. I am a bent twig.

I don't want to make anyone else love my loves. I just want them to let me love them. To love the velvety pansy, my mother's favorite flower. "I love their little kitten faces."

Why must we have a "national" flower? Must we choose?

And if we choose one, how shall we look the others in the face? How apologize to them?

That's where I ended and showed what I had written to my husband.

He said, "You are wrong. You are far too personal. You aren't the nation!

"I was not born in this country, and in that I am like millions of other Americans. But wherever we come from, we find here a sweet familiar face, shining at a wayside and reminding us of our old homes: the wild rose. It is the flower of the world."

"Then give it to the United Nations," I said pettishly.

"America is a United Nations," he said. " 'A race of races and a nation of nations.' The wild rose is everybody's flower. The flower of the native and the immigrant. Some form of it grows everwhere north of the Equator.

"It's an old, old flower, in a young country, inhabited by people who move. Not every flower grows everywhere in America, but outside the deserts the wild rose does.

"I think when the pioneers came and broke the first sod, and then, later, when their descendants began to push and settle west, they had no time at first to plant flowers. They planted potatoes and beans, and wheat and corn. But I can imagine a little girl, coming in from the sunny borders of woods or a rough pasture, saying, 'Look, Mama, isn't it pretty?' and holding in scratched fingers, a branch of wild rose. And I bet her father dug up some of those bushes or vines and planted them near the cabin door, and they were the first American gardens."

"So you think it should be the national flower?"

"Oh, yes," he said. "Definitely. Only the rose."

Observations of
Everyday Life

Occupation: Housewife

A WOMAN of my acquaintance, whom I interrupted while she was filling out an official questionnaire, laid down her pen with a sigh.

"One question on all official or unofficial papers — government, legal, tax, what-not — always gets my goat," she said. "Fills me with an inferiority complex as 'deep as a well and as wide as a barn door.' It's that query: 'Occupation?' And I have to write down 'Housewife.' When I write it I realize that here I am, a middle-aged woman, with a university education, and I've never made *anything* out of my life. I'm just a housewife."

I couldn't help bursting into laughter. "The trouble with you," I said, "is that you have to find one word to cover a dozen occupations, all of which you follow expertly and all more or less simultaneously. You might write: "Business manager, cook, nurse, chauffeur, dressmaker, interior decorator, accountant, caterer, teacher, private secretary — or just put down 'philanthropist.' "

"Philanthropists are people who give away money," she demurred.

"Not in the exact meaning of the word," I countered. "A philanthropist is a person who loves humanity and gives away something for love. All your life you have been giving away your energies, your skills, your talents, your services — for love."

"Not exactly giving them away," she demurred. "I've been supported. And I guess I've been paid with lots of love in return." She looked happier.

"Or you might put down: 'Free woman.' "

"Free?" she countered. "I can hardly call my soul my own."

"Oh, yes you can," I replied firmly, for the woman is a great friend and I know her very well. "And your life has always fulfilled the prime test of a free existence — namely, never to do anything just for money."

"Perhaps you have something there," she smiled. "But here I am, nearly fifty years old, and I have never done what I hoped to do in my youth. Music! I played the piano twenty-five years ago better than I do now. And I had a college education — wasted."

Wasted! Without a mind trained to concentration, to tackling and solving problems, weighing alternative policies, and planning the use of time, this woman never could have done what she has. As for her artistic and intellectual interests —

"But all your children are musical. And that is simply because you brought music into your home — isn't it?"

My friend grinned. "But all this vicarious living — through others." She sighed again.

"As vicarious as Napoleon Bonaparte," I scoffed. "Or a — queen. I simply refuse to share your self-pity. You are one of the most successful women I know."

And I certainly meant it.

This woman married at twenty-one a struggling high school teacher. They went to housekeeping on $35 a week. They had three children — two sons and a daughter. It took her husband twenty-five years to rise high in his profession. During fifteen of those years — until an outstanding and popular historical work brought him to the forefront — they had to live on very modest means with exceptionally refined tastes. Their children were grown before teaching and books won him a quite handsome income. But if this break had never happened, my friend would have been no less a success, for her greatest achievements were performed when her husband was earning between three and five thousand dollars a year. During all that time her husband and family never lived in anything but a well-kept, charming home. They never in their lives ate a bad meal. They were always attractively dressed. All three children were (and are) admired for their good manners and exceptional intelligence and industry — which saved their parents much money, for they were largely educated by scholarships. They were also educated for kindness and consideration, because there was always room for one more in that home, and for several years it was shared with a refugee child.

To do what this woman did with her husband's modest income was a feat of management, showing executive ability of a high order. Her gifts as a craftsman were no less formidable. I once found her papering her living room — "A perfect cinch once you get the hang of it," she remarked happily. As a food buyer she would have won a high salary in any restaurant, for she watched the markets like a hawk, and planned delicious meals accordingly. When the children were small she made all their clothes and most of her own, including suits and topcoats, having gone between housekeeping duties to a tailoring school. In "time off" she typed her husband's manuscripts and proofread every book; played piano duets with the children to make practicing more fun; followed them in their reading when they were in high school, the better to discuss the books under study; and as they grew up and went away to college, threw herself into the work of the community, sat on city housing boards; planned festivals to make up the church deficit; took the lead for better schools; and, in fact, when I think of her solid achievements they are matched by few "career" women.

"But I never earned any money." That is the lament of many "housewives."

If the family is considered as a unit, that is simply not so. Hundreds of thousands of women, all over the United States, are contributing as much to the well-being of their families by the services they render and the brains they mobilize as are their income-earning husbands. Compile the cost of their services, if it had to be paid to half a dozen professionals! And what do most men work for anyhow? They work for their homes! The home they are able to support is the real measure of their financial "success." In that home, expenditure is quite as important as income, and 80 per cent of American income is spent by "housewives," for better or for worse. Who does not know $10,000-income homes that cannot match in order, graciousness, and comeliness, homes run on half that income? Who supplies the economic ability which overcomes income deficiencies? Invariably some "housewife."

Who can hire, at any price, a substitute for a mother? Who can find a housekeeper, who thinks twice about every purchase, weighing value against available cash? On what labor market is affection to be purchased, patient devotion, good humor, laughter?

There is no question that most women can save in the home by their managerial talents more money than they could bring into it from outside work.

How many men would have given up in despair in those troughs of life into which everyone drops at one time or another, had it not been for the patient faith and the carefully concealed sacrifices of a loving wife? That woman of despised occupation!

It seems to me I am continually opening novels about the pretty girl who turns into a slut and a harridan upon marriage; or whose spirit is broken by the boredom of household tasks. Perhaps I know only very nice people, but I know them in all walks of life, and it seems to me that these dismal creatures are the exception not the rule. It is probably true, as Mrs. Virginia Woolf pointed out in "A Room of One's Own," that lack of money of their own, and of leisure, has thwarted the genius of some women. It is true that the most conspicuous women geniuses have been childless, and free from household cares. However, the world and civilization are not made by genius alone, but by civilization's myriad unsung heroes and heroines. And a world full of feminine genius but poor in children would rapidly come to an end.

One might also ask: What would become of the men geniuses? Someone has said, "When you see a great man, you can deduce a great mother." That has been confirmed over and over again, and by great men themselves. But great mothers, like great geniuses, have to work at their task. It isn't just an inborn talent that flourishes without constant effort. And most good men had *good* mothers, too. Children — especially, I think, boy children — usually get their ethical standards, as well as their ambition and their courage, largely from their mothers. The instinct of the masses of the people in Catholic countries, who against the theologians, elevated the Mother of Christ into part of the Godhead — as eloquently told by Henry Adams in *Mont St.-Michel and Chartres* — was a sound one, growing out of human experience. If Christ is perfect, they argued wisely, His Mother is perfect, for only a perfect mother has a perfect son. And so they elevated the gentle and inconspicuous Mary into the Queen of Heaven, and built their loveliest cathedrals to *Notre Dame*, Our Lady.

That may seem a far cry from "Occupation: Housewife." But is it so far? The homemaker, the nurturer, the creator of childhood's environment is the constant re-creator of culture, civilization, and virtue.

Therefore, assuming that she has done and is doing well that great managerial task and creative activity, let her write her occupation proudly, with a flourish: Housewife!

The Little Towns

ALTHOUGH OF LATE YEARS, and for time-saving purposes, I have traveled inside and outside America almost entirely by plane, I love trains. The new ones, particularly west of Chicago, are luxurious with lounges, excellent dining cars, comfortable bedrooms, radios, television sets, and the latest magazines.

I appreciate these increased comforts, but they are not why I love trains. I love them because one can look out of the window, and see the country roll past, slowly enough for the eye to take in many details. From a plane the landscape appears only as an abstract pattern, of geometrically outlined fields and forests, ribbons of roads, clusters of houses, which must be villages, and the lines, lights, squares, and towers of great towns and cities. Often, of course, one sees nothing of human life and movement at all, only banks of cloud, lovely in some lights. But everything is far away, seen from a lofty perspective, not intimate.

This fall and winter a speaking tour took me out to the Middle West — Ohio, Kansas, Minnesota — and to places not easily accessible by air, so I went on trains, fuming, as I started, that so much "time would be lost," and then wondering whimsically what becomes of lost time — wondering to what limbo it is consigned and what it does with itself when it gets there — and recalling, as I so often do, the words of that minor but delightful poet, William Henry Davies:

> *A poor life this if, full of care,*
> *We have no time to stand and stare.*

So I sat and stared, well rewarded, as the colored counties passed my window, noting with satisfaction the many terraced and contoured fields, brown with the stalks of harvested wheat and corn, or emerald with sproutings of winter rye; noting the reflections of the last leaves and of racing clouds in little ponds, designed to hold precious water; admiring the neat white houses, their doorways usually shaded by twin trees, and around them big barns and silos, painted "Indian" red, or sometimes built of flashing aluminum, within neatly fenced barnyards.

But most of all I loved looking at the little towns as we went through. One doesn't see the best aspects of a town from the railroad yards, but as the train pulled in or out, slowing down even if it did not stop, one always had a vista of streets — of "Main Street" where the shops and stores and largest buildings always are, and of the streets where people

live. And, looking down those streets, neatly paved, shaded
by great maples or arching elms, their homes set back among
raked lawns and clumps of shrubbery, I thought, as I have
thought time and again, that nobody knows *anything* about
America who does not know its little towns.

It is all very well to talk of the beauties of our parent-
countries and civilization, Europe. We have few great cities
that for beauty, grace, architecture, or planning compare
favorably with Paris, Rome, Florence, Vienna, Madrid,
Amsterdam, Stockholm, Brussels, or even Berlin, handsome
if not lovely before it came crashing down, or with foggy,
imperial London. The European landing on our shores finds
New York splendid, breathtaking, monumental, exciting, but
with its apparently insoluble transport problem, noisy and
anything but comfortable, and quite incredibly dirty. How
could a city be otherwise which is inhabited by nine million
people, where (in Manhattan, at least) there are no alleys,
and garbage must be collected at front entrances, and streets
cleaned between rows of parked cars?

Washington is a handsome city but a cold one, a "company
town" devoted only to government, extraordinarily lacking
in metropolitan amenities, even to numbers of first-rate restaurants, and containing in immediate juxtaposition to the
finest residential areas many slums.

Chicago, perennially ill-governed, handsome in parts, vital
and exciting always, can challenge all contenders with the
extent of its constantly encroaching slums.

America, I think, is worst represented in its great cities,
and these are what the foreigner usually sees — noting the
dirt, the noise, the slums jostling the boulevards, and the terribly high rentals for tiny apartments.

But for comfort, cleanliness, comeliness, coziness, few, if
any, countries can match the American small town — from

New England to California, from the Gulf of Mexico to the Canadian border, taking them *as a whole*.

There are exquisite English, French, and Italian villages to which the tourist is directed by Baedeker. But there are also thousands that are unspeakably dreary, with streets of dark, uncomfortable homes set wall to wall flush with the sidewalk, without lawns, and, except for public parks, hardly a tree. Life, too, in them is provincial and inbred to an extent that it no longer is in the American small town. "Gopher Prairie" is not "the climax of civilization," as it was not when Sinclair Lewis so dubbed it with ironic scorn in his introduction to *Main Street*. But Carol Kennicott, whose frustrated discontent is the subject of the famous novel, would find much more stimulation and sophistication today in Gopher Prairie than she did less than a generation ago.

In the Middle West, the architecture seldom has the grace and proportion observable in New England, Virginia, and the early-settled states, where Georgian influences still predominate. The Middle West grew up when wood-fretted gables, towers and porte-cocheres made a "mansion," when verandas were thrown out in all directions, and the *ne plus ultra* was a window of quite hideously gaudy red-blue-and-green glass on the stairs. The age of golden oak, black walnut, Brussels carpets, lace curtains, whatnots, center tables, and bead curtains. Many of these houses are left, as I saw from the train, passing through Ohio and Kansas, and one of the finest collections of them I have ever seen is in Van Wert, Ohio, population 14,000, where I stopped to speak. There, too, the old Marsh mansion, now hostess house for a school for maladjusted children, founded and endowed by the Marsh family, is probably the best extant museum of the period.

I confess that these houses delight me. I remember them from my childhood in upstate New York, as the homes of my father's wealthier parishioners or friends. Whatever they lacked of grace, they did not lack space and stability. They were built for big families, in which every member had a room of his own which was not a cubicle. They had parlors for the grownups and guests, sitting rooms where the children played in blizzardy weather, big dining rooms, which were often the family sitting rooms — and how many problems in compound-fractions, or "essays" on geography, have I not done under the hanging lamp over the dining room table! They had attics full of trunks, storing two or three generations of old clothes to dress up in. If it rained one could ride a tricycle on the wide verandas. And they also had "hired girls," and even occasionally uniformed maids. Perhaps I like them now as an amusing break in too standardized "good taste."

But looking down the streets of the little towns, I saw that the newer homes are small and "labor-saving" — for the hired girl has vanished — but still with much more space outside and in than any but the rich can afford in big cities. Some are the ranch type, low, wide, and wide-windowed, but most are two-storied, or a story-and-a-half, with dormers and usually with front porches, on which often stand bicycles or tricycles. One can trace the growth of the family by looking at the houses, the "Ell" that had obviously been added, the dormer that plainly had not originated with the house. Some of the owners, I saw in passing, had in an outbreak of rugged individualism, defied the prevailing white or white and green, and painted their little houses — whatever the architecture — pink, or robin's-egg blue, or gray with blue shutters, and they sang to me. And always the lawns, with never a hedge or fence against a neighbor, and always the noble American trees.

(I wished I could be taking some important Russian — incognito, in a false mustache — along with me, to show him what *community*, as contrasted with communism, can be; to show him the wonderful friendliness of small-town America, where nobody is an anonymous cipher.)

And also to show him what "progress" and "advance" manifests itself in the little towns that metropolitan Americans still call "the sticks." Despite the continued growth of our great cities, and apart from the millions of Americans living on farms, nearly 42,000,000 of our people live in "the sticks," in towns or cities of under 50,000.

How does today's Main Street differ from the one described in Sinclair Lewis's famous novel of 1920?

Like Sinclair Lewis, I was also born and brought up in little towns of the period he described, and I never could quite agree with the picture he presented. But even that ironic satirist would change it, were he to write today. As a speaker, I have of late years visited every state in the union but one, and spoken in hundreds of small towns — invited by a Chamber of Commerce, a woman's club, a local college, a public forum, or some other civic group, and not to entertain an audience but to speak very seriously about American problems, foreign and domestic. This in itself indicates a change — a shift to a far wider range of interest. I have spoken in towns of 5000 and upward, always rejoicing when my schedule gave me a free day in which to meet people and look around. And if there are any small towns without *proportionately* as many civilized, informed, public-spirited, and wide-awake people as there are in the great cities, I haven't been in them. Their local civic consciousness, I think, is higher than that of the Big City populations. In the great cities people vote for reforms. In the little towns they *undertake* the reforms. And the old provincial tightness is disappearing.

Almost all Americans, whatever their so-called "social station," travel today to surrounding big cities, and often from one end of the country to another. Hundreds of thou-

sands have been abroad. A physician in a village of 2000
whom I had to consult about my throat wished to discuss
China. He was born in China, his missionary father having
gone from this same small town. The son lived there to the
age of fourteen, speaks several Chinese dialects, was sent
home to be educated and then returned as a member of U.S.
Intelligence. While he swabbed out my throat he told me
more about China — very precisely, chapter and verse —
than I could learn from much reading.

"Why did you decide to settle here?"

"I like it — several of us are starting a little clinic — it's
needed — nice place to live — nice people."

A garage owner told me about spending last summer in
Italy. And so it goes.

People in the small towns read. "What do you think of
Dewhurst's article on the Russians in the October twenty-
ninth issue of *U.S. News and World Report?*" a Kansas
rancher asked. I had missed the article in my travels. He outlined the contents and I promised to look it up when I got
back, recommending in turn the book by the Englishman,
Edward Crankshaw, *Cracks in the Kremlin Wall.* He made
a note of it, after which we talked about Soil Conservation,
of which he is a master and an enthusiast.

I ran into friends of friends. A lady who has a quite fab-
ulous china and gift shop in Salem, Ohio, and knows all about
Austrian and Swiss toys, Bohemian glass, and the merits and
demerits of English, German, American, French, and Italian
porcelain and ceramics, inquired about friends who are my
neighbors in Vermont. We wrote them a mutually signed
postcard, and I had made a new and charming friend — only
one of many.

The spontaneous kindness of small-town people to the
visitor, the warm way they take one into their homes and
hearts, their interest and curiosity about places they have not

seen, or topics they confess they "haven't given much thought to," are surely unique to this country. I am ever reminded of Walt Whitman's tribute to America:

Here is the hospitality which forever indicates heroes.

The interest of small-town folks in the national and international scene is, of course, much more platonic than their interest in their own state and community. How, or why, should it be otherwise? The world is too big for many of us to love. Even America is too big really to *love* except as an abstraction. American patriotism, I have come to think, is the accumulation of thousands of little patriotisms. The Vermonter, the Kansan, the Virginian, the Ohioan — I choose at random — still seems to believe as he did in Lewis' time, that all America revolves around his state, the state around his town, and that his is the best state and the best town in the nation. But the new value of this attitude is that he tries his best to make it so! It is not just vainglory.

"Main Street," the commercial part of the small towns, is, indeed, greatly standardized throughout the country. One sees the same supermarkets, dime-to-dollar and drug stores everywhere, many of them chains. The contents of the stores and shops (and also their prices) are pretty uniform. The "Brand" has taken over.

But the small-towner is eagerly prideful of what sets his town *apart* — and he is proudest, I have found, of its social and civic achievements.

Nearly every town I visit has something that is the "biggest" in America (or the world) and its citizens will tell you so, usually with a grin and the preface of "Believe it or not . . ." Van Wert has in its Borden cheese factory "the largest in the world," unique in that it alone produces the famous Liederkranz, America's only original contribution to the soft fermented cheeses favored by gourmets. I was enchanted to learn that the Swiss immigrant who created it did so by sheer chance, that all of Borden's laboratory technicians have never been able to isolate the bacteria which make it in twenty-four days of curing; that the coy bacteria reside in the wooden racks and bamboo mats where the cheese is ripened; that the management therefore (apologetically) can't use stainless steel; and that every ounce of the process of making it has to be performed by hand. (It enchants me, along with the cheese, because I like to think that a few good things defy the chemists.)

In Pratt, Kansas, population 8000, one is quickly told that here are the greatest fresh-water fish hatcheries (started by an ingenious nature-lover originally, but now operated by the state) in America or the world, along with the finest museum of Kansan wild life. (It's a honey.)

And Pratt is also the largest manufacturer of fly swatters!

But having disposed of the "biggest and best," citizens want to show or tell you of the projects created by the community: the new schools, the hospital, the clinics, the amateur symphony orchestra, the Little Theater, the beautiful churches, the public forum, the public swimming pool, the lovely park and recreation grounds, the youth clubs. Mr. Babbitt is still boosting but he's a different Babbitt boosting different things. And while he shows you around he wants to discuss the course of American education and how to deal with juvenile delinquency. "We have not had a single case of juvenile crime in this community in four years," a citizen told me. "We used to have some. But we put our minds on it, and I think we've done a pretty good job. We think our kids are about as happy and good as you'll find anywhere."

Who does all these things in the little towns — things that are transforming them?

As far as I can learn, nearly everybody. Once the most "important" people in the community were the ones with the most money, even if they were mean as old Scrooge. Now a well-to-do man who is not also public-spirited goes without acclaim. So, of course, he becomes public-spirited even if not naturally gifted, one might say, in that direction. Not only because it's good business but because every human person wants to be admired, and if possible loved, by his fellow men.

You can't be loved in America's little towns if you set yourself above others. Very rich people live in little towns, but they don't have butlers. Even if they could get them, it wouldn't be "in style." It is "in style" to entertain informally — and casserole cooking is becoming an art. It is "in style" for the mistress of a very beautiful and obviously expensive home to bring the roast beef out of her stainless steel kitchen, where she has cooked it herself, for her husband to carve and pass around, and for her guests to help stack the dishwasher afterwards. Carol Kennicott's prediction that dishes would one day be washed by machinery has been realized. Nor could she, today, with the same accuracy, criticize the lack of social consciousness.

It is "in style" for a busy young banker to coach a kid's football team. It is "in style" for the son of a pioneer whose father amassed a fortune in the nineties to turn his great inherited house into a recreation center. It's "in style" to care about others.

Industries are moving to the small towns, and they are different too from what they were twenty-five years ago. No longer are they eyesores. They, too, stand amidst lawns and shrubbery. They aren't belching smoke to blacken the countryside, and often they look more like private schools than like factories.

Small-town folks are far more sophisticated, cultivated, and knowledgeable than were Carol Kennicott's neighbors, partly because everybody has more money, because travel has been democratized, and because radio and television bring the affairs of the world into every living room. Small-towners are as familiar with the faces of Broadway actors as are New Yorkers. The "elocutionists" they go to the nearest big town to hear are Charles Laughton, Raymond Massey, Judith Anderson, and the others who have made a new dramatic art of reading. They travel sixty miles to listen to a symphony concert and return the same night. They follow the panel discussions on television — and participate in them afterward.

"Just the same, the most talented small-towners head for the cities," a small-towner himself reminded me.

This is true and it is natural. The greatly gifted are usually restless, and want to test and match their talents in a larger room. But small towns (and smaller cities) have nevertheless produced almost all of our leading native-born writers and other artists. Of America's four winners of the Nobel Prize for Literature, Sinclair Lewis, Eugene O'Neill, Pearl Buck, and William Faulkner, all but O'Neill, who was born and educated in Ireland, came originally from small towns, though Pearl Buck was brought up as a missionary's child in China. Lewis, a perpetual wanderer, lived in many parts of the United States and died in Rome, but his work was always centered in "Gopher Prairie" and "Zenith." And he willed that his ashes should be interred in Sauk Center. Faulkner has never moved, except temporarily, farther from his birthplace, New Albany in Mississippi, than to Oxford, in the same state.

American writers of established international reputation have come almost without exception from small towns or small cities — Carl Sandburg, Willa Cather, Ernest Hemingway, John Steinbeck, Thomas Wolfe, Edna St. Vincent Millay, Maxwell Anderson, Erskine Caldwell, Tennessee Williams. Even the highly sophisticated Scott Fitzgerald, for whom there is a new vogue, was born and brought up not in a great metropolis but in St. Paul, Minnesota.

It has recently been said (by Professor Lewis Atherton) that it is hard to find philosophical interests anywhere in the Middle West. It is hard to find them in small towns. But it is certainly just as hard, proportionately, to find them anywhere else. Our century is not devoted to philosophy but to technology. The latter is not quite so overwhelming in the smaller places.

Carol Kennicott, who revolted against Main Street and her prairie town was no genius and no philosopher. Essentially she was a yearner, just a little brighter, more literate, more romantic, and more aspiring — to she never knew just what — than her neighbors; more bored than profoundly rebellious. And eventually, you may remember, she went back home. Now, twenty-five years later, we hazard the guess that she never would have left. There is too much going on. Not enough for most people of genius, but plenty for the Carol Kennicotts.

Can Women Be Ladies?

A NEWSPAPER ADVERTISEMENT of a "foundation garment" recently attracted my somewhat startled attention by announcing that it would give its wearer "the only *fashionable* look, the only *possible* look . . . the ladylike look."

Good gracious, I thought to myself, is the ideal of the lady about to be revived?

I confess that I was puzzled as to how one such garment or another could contribute to making a girl or woman appear to be more or less of a lady. I suppose — from the description, which promises to make one subtly beautiful — that it is not a garment designed to emphasize, enhance, or call exaggerated attention to the physical endowments associated with sex and "the sweater girl." Such garments, particularly bras, have catered to the long-current trend of making the most of the female bosom, or even of building one in if nature has not sumptuously endowed, and the advertisers have intimated the "sexy" effect of their wares. Could it be, I ruminated, that a too obvious sexiness of appearance is about to become *unfashionable?*

Well, I don't know. What I do know is that, with the exception of certain religious sects, women, whether ladies or not, have always tried to make the most of their natural endowments, and to improve on nature with art, though fashion is a whimsical thing, and has an extraordinary power to create and undo ideals of erotic beauty. It has made the "boyish" figure modish, designing clothes to eliminate the waist, compress the hips, and flatten the bosom; it has decreed skirt-lengths from knees to ankles; it has hobbled women into tight sheaths, and split these sheaths to expose glimpses of enticing legs; or it has corseted the waist to such breathlessness that no wonder Victorian ladies were perpetually swooning. From steelbound waists it has pushed up bosoms to resemble bouquets erupting from slender vases; it has draped the ladies in Grecian folds, or surrounded them with the swirling skirts of peasants; it has topped them with mountainous hairdos, exposed their fore-

heads or covered them with bangs, or cut their locks to resemble the head of a medieval page, or of an Italian gamin, or
of a poodle.

And by and large, the Captain's Lady and Judy O'Grady
have gone along, starving themselves when the mode called
for extreme thinness and fattening themselves (in happier
modes) and always, always painting their faces, shadowing
their eyes to make them appear larger, and reddening their
mouths.

Not long ago, in Egypt, I visited some excavations around
the oldest of the pyramids, from which I learned that 9000
years ago women, certainly classed in their day as "ladies,"
used eye shadow, mascara, rouge, and lipstick. And always
they have perfumed and bejeweled themselves.

Modesty of dress and deportment has, however, been associated with the greatest "ladies," namely, royalty.

One cannot imagine either of the two living Queens of
England — the Queen Mother and Elizabeth II — or the
Queens of Holland or the Scandinavian countries dressed to
call attention to their sexual attributes. Their clothes are
beautiful, but conform to no exaggerations of fashion — nor
do they set the standards of fashion. Their figures are natural
— as natural as their exquisite manners, and they do set the
standard of good manners, considerate, delicate, and unre-
strained. Like Caesar's wife's, their virtue is, and must be,
above suspicion. Divorce and, of course, scandal, are out of
the question for any twentieth-century sovereign who will
retain the throne.

But that was not always true.

Catherine of Russia was a great queen, but her morals were
notorious. She was quite unashamed about them, too, not
even paying the tribute of hypocrisy, which vice so often
pays to virtue, nor among the intimates of her court was she

modest in any way. A great sovereign, she was certainly in modern terms no lady.

But what *is a lady?* (You see to what extent one's thoughts can be led by contemplation of a simple advertisement!)

The *Encyclopaedia Britannica* devotes 7½ lines to define "lady" in two applications: as a title of nobility correlative to "Lord," and as the correlative of "gentleman." It devotes about 2 pages to describing the male correlatives of lady, but still leaves "lady" pretty indefinite, since, as James Branch Cabell remarked in "Something about Eve," "No lady is ever a gentleman"!

We are not concerned with "lady" as a title of nobility. There are no American Lady-Lords. "Gentleman" is not a title, though the word (or concept) has had an interesting evolution. In its original meaning a gentleman was a man of good family, belonging, in the Latin *gentilis* to a distinguishable race, or gens. "Those whom their race and blood or *at least their virtues*, make noble and known." There seems always to have been this dual association. A man of noble birth was accepted as a "gentleman," unless his behavior contradicted it. A story is attributed to James II of England, who, when a mother entreated him to "make my son a gentleman," replied, "Madam, I could make him a nobleman by giving him a title but God Almighty could not make him a gentleman." In short, a gentleman is created not by a King or a title, nor by birth, but by his behavior.

In the days before there were conscript armies, a development of democracy unknown before the French Revolution, those who bore arms for their country were considered of superior social rank, their families distinguished by having "a coat of arms" to signalize the fact — a habit that made fortunes for the heralds who designed them. Shakespeare was turned by grant of a coat of arms from a "vagabond" into a "gentleman." In the fourteenth and fifteenth centuries fighting was apparently the sole honorable profession for gentlemen — but Joan of Arc, who fought in those times, was never considered a "lady."

"Gentleman" has gone through a wide, democratic revolution. Already, in Shakespeare's day, all in the learned professions — clergy, lawyers, scholars — were considered "gentlemen." But a learned woman could not have been a lawyer, nor her desire to be one the aspiration of a lady. In 1815 the *Encyclopaedia Britannica* described a gentleman as anyone who without title bears a coat of arms or whose ancestors have been freemen. By 1845 all above the rank of yeomen (free farmers) could be regarded as gentlemen, and by 1856 the title was accorded all persons above the rank of "common tradesman" "when their manners are indicative of a certain amount of refinement and intelligence."

Until fairly recently trade was not considered an appropriate occupation for a gentleman. Buying and selling were thought inconducive to the development of culture or character. But all these considerations of professional activities or engagement, never applicable to women, have gradually faded. Position, education, and unaffectedly good manners, still mark the gentleman in any society, but the term also involves a superior standard of conduct, related to self-respect, honorable dealings — "his word is as good as his bond."

"The gentleman owes his acceptance as such, not to circumstances but to his behavior in them," one historian records.

We may assume, therefore, that a lady must possess sufficient education or culture to enable her to converse grammatically and in a pleasant voice above the level of idle, personal gossip; that under whatever circumstances she lives, she conducts a home with a degree of refinement; and that she conforms to a superior standard of conduct.

And, yet, despite the increased equality between the sexes, the standards "becoming to a gentleman" are still not always consistent with those "becoming to a lady." What society finds acceptable in a gentleman is not equally acceptable in a gentlewoman — or lady.

For to men (who have written innumerable books, romances, and poetry about woman) she still appears in a dual light. She is the eternal seductress and temptress leading men to evil; the Eve who lost for Adam paradise. And she is the angel, Goethe's "eternal feminine" who "leads us ever upward."

She is considered either infinitely worse than man, or infinitely better. Her influence for good or evil over man is vastly greater — or so the poets have always thought — than man's influence over her.

She need not be as brilliant, educated, or even creatively as intelligent as man. But she must be *more* virtuous than man usually is, or she will ruin him and the race.

I gather this from reading what men (and some women) have written about "woman" from the ancient Greeks to the present day. And I also gather that "woman" is a subject far more mysterious, frustrating, and interesting than "man."

Burton Stevenson's *The Home Book of Quotations: Classical and Modern*, devotes 30 two-column finely printed pages to quotations of what great and lesser poets, philosophers, and sages have said about WOMAN, and additional pages to Maids, Virgins, and Girls, but fills only 18 with what they have said about man — including under "Man," mankind as such! Far more attention has been paid to her than to Wisdom or War. And in the sum of this concentrated interest, little concern is expressed for woman as a lady. She is "the weaker sex, to piety more prone," according to William Alexander. Edmund Burke considered her "but an animal and an animal not of the

highest order." But she has also been called "a temple sacred
by birth, and built of hands divine." She is pictured as utterly
frivolous and mysteriously wise. She is the one creature on
whom man can depend, but inconstancy is the essence of her
nature. "Even to vice they are not constant," said Shakespeare
of women in *Cymbeline,* commenting further that:

> *For there's no motion*
> *That tends to vice in man, but I affirm*
> *It is the woman's part; be it lying, note it,*
> *The woman's; flattering, hers; deceiving, hers;*
> *Lust and rank thoughts, hers, hers; revenges, hers . . .*

But Milton, in *Paradise Lost,* called her "the last and best
of all God's works," and Shakespeare, himself, made Portia
the very embodiment of justice and mercy.

Whatever she is or isn't, the poets have tended to regard
her, for better or worse, as an elemental force, far harder to
tame and civilize than is man. "Women will be the last thing
civilized by man," said George Meredith, in *The Ordeal of
Richard Feverel.* She has been likened to "wars and trouble-
some cattle." Dryden found women "not compris'd in our
laws of friendship; they are ferae naturae (in a wild state of
nature)." Kipling found that "The female of the species is
more deadly than the male." Created from a rib of Adam
and not from his head, she is made to be commanded by men
— since the head commands. But since Adam was made of
dirt in the first place and she of man, she is an advanced and
superior work of creation — goodness, how many words, in
prose or rhyme, have been devoted to *that* theme! She is, in
short, man's greatest blessing and greatest curse.

Now, one wonders how such an elemental force of nature
— for good or for evil — can ever be made, or make herself,
into the pale image of a Lady!

After reading reams about woman, I decided she'd better just be woman — a gentlewoman, if possible, with what attributes of a gentleman the viewpoints, desires, imagery, mythology, and prejudices of men will permit her. She can be sure that if she is chaste, men will call her cold; if she is brilliant, men will call her "like a man"; if she is witty they will suspect her virtue; if she is beautiful they will try to annex her as an asset to their own position; if she has executive abilities they will fear her dominance. If she was originally created out of Adam's rib, Adam's successors have been making her up out of their heads ever since.

There is a myth that women never displayed capacity for governing, and were never educated until the nineteenth century, when they began to be emancipated.

I hate to bring the matter up — it seems tactless to men — but the first emancipation of women was effected in the early Middle Ages, when some women emancipated themselves from sex and children and went into religious conventual orders. There some of them, elected by a secret vote of the Sisters, became Abbesses, governing very large communities, self-sufficient in every detail, commanding vast organized charities, hospitals, and primary and secondary educational activities. Sometimes they presided over joint houses of monks and nuns, as at Whitby in England, and Fontevrault, in France. These Abbesses were great executives and as learned theologians as the Abbots. In England they attended the Ecclesiastical Councils. An Abbess in the thirteenth century had great power. And it was devoted entirely to the service of "Our Lady" and her Son.

I think that today if woman desires for her own sake to be a lady — gentle, considerate, fair, and kind — she will have to be so by her own efforts, without the aid of the gentlemen, who can manage to be gentlemen and still prefer blondes.

For, alas, great gentlemen have often dallied with, and sometimes married, women who were no ladies, though in the long run, if they can stick it out, the ladies often hold or get back their gentlemen.

And, if for a change the gentlemen tend to prefer ladies in the first place — and I would think it a pleasant change — women, whatever their natural predilections, will oblige. They will wear shiningly washed hair, simply dressed; they will throw out the musky perfumes and return to mignonette and Parma violets; they will enhance their charms by the most subtle concealment of them; they will lower their voices; they will retreat from advances; they will assume a mien of gentle pride, mind their manners, and be known for their sexual morality and their good works.

For whatever Gentlemen may prefer, Women prefer men — Gentlemen, if possible, but anyhow men. They aim to please. For most of them the object — yes, even, in these emancipated days — is matrimony.

There is no lady whose eye does not gleam, however discreetly, in the presence of an eligible man.

For women are always on their way about the race, especially when men seem so hell-bent to decimate or destroy it. It is not a bad thing to be on one's way about. The function gives them the name. "Woman — a far nobler name than Lady," said the medieval minnesinger, Walther von der Vogelweide.

"What are you going to be when you grow up?" I once asked a little girl of seven.

"I am going to be a lady with a baby," she said with great dignity.

Now, she is grown; she is a lady and has a baby. But I think the baby always had the priority over the lady.

The Sophisticates Are
Not the Wise

WHEN THE HISTORY of these times is seen in retrospect, posterity may marvel that human civilization and culture were brought to the edge of the abyss, not by the simple but by the sophisticated, not by the uneducated but by educated men whose contempt for "old-fashioned" values blinded them to some of the most obvious facts of life.

The sophisticated mind surveys an issue from all sides, and is discontented with every proposed solution, since none corresponds to the "ideal." On the other hand, the sophisticated mind is also capable of rationalizing every thesis pro and con. "There is much to be said on both sides," the mental sophisticate argues, and then proceeds to say it, charmed with his own polemic and his control over words whose meaning it is so easy to distort by subtle shadings and associations. He is like a brilliant lawyer, willing to take the case for or against the defendant and to argue either, with equally brilliant facility, without actually committing himself to either thesis.

For this is the further characteristic of the sophisticate: he does not renounce public discussion to retire into contemplative struggle with the truth. He actively (and influentially) participates in it, contributing to sway simpler minds, in this direction or another. But he never assumes moral leadership, because moral leadership demands the taking of personal responsibility and the making of personal decisions and choices. The mental sophisticate, firmly anchored in mid-air, avoids such decisions, and regards their avoidance as a sign of peculiar superiority. The world is so beneath him, he feels, that he will not stoop to decisions on *its* level. *His* decisions, he inferentially implies, are in a realm inaccessible to the ordinary mind, in a world of the "ideal."

A distinguished and rather involved and esoteric novelist, who nevertheless has taken considerable part in public political discussions, was asked some time ago, "How do you stand on Communism?" He replied, with considerable aplomb, "I am not a Communist nor an anti-Communist."

The awed interviewer of the VIP author did not presume to follow this up with the obvious question, "What the dickens *are* you?" though the question would have been most pertinent. For the writer — whose name is irrelevant, since I present him here as illustrative of a type rather than as a personality — has, in his lifetime, eloquently pleaded the cause of national conservatism, valiantly championed the civil liberties of anti-liberty Communists, and vehemently attacked the right of civil liberties of Fascists. It would therefore have been no adequate answer had he replied, "I am an artist," for (except for the command of an inimitable style) there has been nothing of Art in his political intervention-isms, for or against this cause or that one, and on no higher level than that of more ordinary special pleaders. He has simply — while participating in the struggle — reserved for himself the special privilege as an artist to stand aloof, and to influence others, without himself being compelled to take a stand. This, which calls itself superiority, is actually a com-bination of arrogance and irresponsibility, of pride and cow-ardice, and it accounts for the decline of the faith of simple men in intellect per se, for a cynical attitude toward art and the artist, for a distrust of the educated, and for a growing primitivism and barbarism.

For the function of the artist is not to avoid judgment, but, as a great and thoroughly responsible artist, Walt Whitman, averred, to *be* judgment — judging, "not as the judge judges, but as light, falling around a helpless thing."

The simple mind, unconfused by the pyrotechnics of its own ratiocinations, and living in life, not in some vague ideal, knows that it is impossible to be neither a Communist nor an anti-Communist, and be at the same time a morally responsible man. For Communism throws down an inescapable challenge. Communism does not argue; it states. It does not suggest discussion and compromise; it says, "He who is not for us is against us." It demands Unconditional Surrender — Unconditional Surrender of whole peoples and of every individual mind and soul — and it demands this surrender with a gun in its hand.

Now, there come some — the sophisticated and finicky — who say, "But look at our own society. Can one call it a 'true' democracy? Is there universal justice? Do all minorities within it enjoy equal freedom? Is there not evil everywhere, and on both sides? Must we not clean up our own house before we take a stand against others?"

This attitude reminds me of a Jewish story. A man coming home and finding his house burning to the ground clapped his hands, danced with glee, and cried, "Now those bed bugs are getting it!"

Or of the Irish story: A man is held up by a gunman who demands, "Your money or your life!" He replies, "Take my life; I am saving my money for my old age."

They are like a patient who, informed that he has cancer, argues against an operation on the ground that if he had perfect health, he wouldn't have got cancer, so decides to postpone treating the cancer until his teeth have been repaired.

The struggle in which the twentieth century is engaged is not a mere "ideological" struggle in the mind, fought with words, or to be banished with words. It is a struggle fought with deeds, demanding moral decisions which, in turn, imply actions — as all moral decisions do. The systematic organization of conspiratorial groups for subversion and sabotage, in every country; the organization of great armies, equipped with every modern weapon, to invade and capture weak republics, adding each new conquest to their physical and brachial strength under single- minded leadership — these are not figments of the imagination. They are facts — not occurring in the realm of idea, alone or even primarily, but in the realm of will — the will to power, and the decision to use power.

In the face of that fact and challenge, the sophisticates of the West have infected the whole of our society with their own occupational disease, which is *lack of will.* Unable to make up their own complicated minds (which would require a definite uncompromising choice), they have confused simpler (and wiser and more honest) minds, until the whole West has been like King Canute "who thought by talking to the waves, he could keep back the sea."

Where they should have counseled building dykes, they have counseled letting the sea seek its own level — the while this political and military sea rises to the level of the highest mountain of Tibet, and seeps into the cellars of Greenwich Village, the penthouses of Park Avenue, the faculty chairs of American universities, and the counsels of government.

And simple men, listening for a great voice to fulfill the poet's eternal function and affirm Faith and Resistance, and man's noble, if tragic, destiny, hear little except that life is a mess anyhow, and one thing about as bad as another, or, as the artist Matisse remarked, "Painting a church — it's the same as painting a dance hall." Until these simple men, who do not of themselves confound simple faith with simplicity, finally prefer to turn to barbarous leaders, who, at least, are men of will.

The confusion of intellectualism with intellect, of argument with judgment, of sophistication with wisdom, of rationalization with reason, of a "humanitarianism" that defends every criminal, with the humanism that protects goodness and truth — this confusion is the malaise of our times.

And it is these sophisticates, neither for nor against Communism — nor God, nor Love, nor Truth, nor Duty, nor Faith — who far more than conscious Communist agents have undermined the moral bastions of this country and of all the countries of the West.

They have not even had the wit to recognize their own mortal enemies. For the totalitarian world has no use whatever for sophisticates.

In a healthy, free, and unmenaced society they are its entertainers and its wits. They have their function. But it is not the function of leadership, direct or behind the scenes as wire-pullers and ghost writers for puppets. Theirs is not the function of a true nobility, which every society, however democratic, requires. For the essence of nobility is that it makes decisions, accepts responsibility, and commits itself to the preservation of society and the defense of its greatest values.

The great mind is a complicated mind that evercomes its complications in silent responsible struggle, fusing their rainbow colors into the limpid light of Truth so clear that the simplest mind sees, welcomes, and understands it.

The Great Mind writes a Gettysburg Address, and the words are at one and the same time Word and Act, Thought and Will. On the highest level the word returns to God, and is God.

But it is never the word of a sophisticate.

The Twelve-foot Ceiling

IN A RECENT publication I read an interview with the famous architect Frank Lloyd Wright, occasioned by the unwrapping of his model for The Modern Gallery of Nonobjective Painting. In the course of the interview he called the big gray Metropolitan Museum of Art "undemocratic." Public rooms, he explained, should be only about twelve feet high, so the people will not feel "insignificant."

Mr. Wright is a lover and builder of architecture on broad horizontal lines, and in his designs has contributed much to the comfort, beauty, and practicality of domestic life. He also said many intelligent things about city planning. When Rockefeller Center was under discussion, he suggested that it would be better to tear down what was there and plant the space to grass and trees. But I wonder whether he wanted only twelve-foot trees, lest the people, beside a towering elm, should feel "insignificant."

The Metropolitan Museum leaves much to be desired, but not because its rooms are lofty. The GI Joes whom I saw standing awe-stricken in the great nave of Salisbury Cathedral; or watching the robed procession in Canterbury slowly climb the vast flight of stairs which leads from nave to altar, for the enthronement of the archbishop; or kneeling under the lofty arches of Notre-Dame de Paris; or gazing with saddened, awe-struck eyes into the wreckage of St. Michael's in Munich; or staring upward, in St. Peter's, at Michelangelo's dome were not feeling insignificant. On the contrary, they were realizing that life had a grandeur, beauty, and significance above and beyond themselves in which, nevertheless, they could share. The recognition did not demean but expanded them, not in self-satisfaction but in esteem for the possibilities in human achievement.

The terrible heresy of modern democratism is to confound democracy with mediocrity. This is to make the "common man" into the modern tyrant. Everything, it is argued, must be keyed and toned down to his understanding, lest he get an "inferiority complex." Books must be written in the language of the gutter. Motion pictures must not appeal "above a mental age of eleven years." The height of inspiration should be put at twelve feet — twice the measure of a tall man; one must not expect him to lift his eyes beyond double his own stature!

This neodemocratism has nothing to do with democracy, nor was it invented by common men, but by panderers who wish to divest the people of their own personalities and make them into masses. You can search America, like Diogenes with his lantern, and you are not likely to find a single American who will describe himself as a member of the masses. The masses exist as the offspring of modern industrial civilization and commercialism, with their many errors and crimes, but the business of democracy is to turn them into The People again. Every girl or boy, be he a mechanic's child or a hod carrier's, in every moment of intellectual, emotional or spiritual awakening, wants to become something other than of the mass; wants to *be*, in full consciousness of personal, individual existence as something different, apart and therefore precious. He does not want a ceiling put over his life. He says, "The sky's the limit."

Every child wants to adore. His father — what schoolboy fights occur if one boy says to another, "Your dad's no good." What childish woe is more tragic than loss of confidence in father or in mother? The human being responds to what is above, not beneath him: to the father as the symbol of strength; to the mother, as the symbol of virtue; to the bigger boy; to the girl who is "better than I am." Out of this comes spiritual growth.

The farm lad lies on the hillside and gazes at the fleecy clouds floating in the faraway blueness, or on a starry night identifies red Antares or blue Arcturus from its relationship to the Big Dipper; he loves the broadest, tallest maple tree in the farmyard, and brags that it has stood there for a hundred and fifty years; he loves the ballads of prowess, of which the American folklore is so full — Paul Bunyan, the Gargantuan. He is ever conscious of the danger and grandeur of the elements — of the shattering thunder, and the torrential rain, and the pullets that will drown unless rescued from the range; of the sun calling the earth to fruition or baking the earth on the roots of crops; of his own inadequacy, often, to do more than endure. He does not learn from Nature that the universe revolves around himself, and at his own rhythm, and to suit his own whims, but that it continually invites him to expand himself into it, mastering, if he can, flood and drought, tempest and storm, and enduring with fortitude what is beyond him to master. That is probably one reason why farm boys grow up to contribute so many names to *Who's Who*, as inventors, scientists, scholars, educators, artists, and managers of great industries.

The measure of a man is never the ceiling of his smug self-satisfaction, but the measure of his humility and reverence, which do not demean but ennoble, and are hallmarks of all noble natures. And the great apostles of American democracy wanted to lift the ceilings, not clamp them down.

Thomas Jefferson, America's first great democrat, lived in what was, in European terms, a wilderness. But he was antiwilderness and pro-civilization and culture. He did not build himself a log cabin, but "Monticello," a large, beautiful mansion; nor did he think the aspirations of the country should be limited to the aspirations of the average. He did not believe in horizontal education; he proposed an educacational system whereby all children would be given the education for which their talents fitted them. They would start equal — he never expected they would finish equal, for he was too accurate an observer of nature. He was a slaveholder who hated slavery and believed the slaveholders should abolish it, since the slaves obviously could not. He did not go and live in his slaves' cabins, but recognizing the extraordinary musical talent of the colored people, brought them into his great house, and organized them into an orchestra, and taught them to play Mozart.

Emerson, a philosopher of American democracy, did not advocate a twelve-foot ceiling, but said, "Hitch your wagon to a star." He knew the wagon would never reach the stars. But the height to which a man ascends is commensurate to his ambition; set his ceiling at twelve feet and eventually he will be living underground.

If the limits of art are to be set in advance by the tape measure of mediocre appreciation, by and by we shall have no more art. The essence of art is that it is unique and distinguished — the expression of the most creative moment of a uniquely creative talent and personality. It is begotten of sensitive and humble appreciation of the greatness, not the littleness, of life; of the eternal wonder of birth, death, and love; of insight into great laws of rhythm and form, point and counterpoint, in color and sound. It exalts not men but Man, not at the average but at his most creative and Godlike.

All great art — a Beethoven symphony, a Michelangelo or Giotto fresco, a Hamlet or King Lear, the Psalms of David, a Brothers Karamazov of Dostoyevsky — creates in the beholder not self-satisfaction but wonder and awe. Its great liberation is to lift us out of ourselves.

In London, when the National Gallery reopened after V-E Day, and only thirty or forty of the very greatest of its pictures were taken from their wartime cellars to hang upon its walls, I watched my husband before a little picture by Rembrandt that he had long known from reproductions but saw now for the first time, in the original. Pale with excitement, and unconscious of the surrounding visitors, he stood motionless for half an hour, murmuring, "It's a miracle — a miracle." Why is it a miracle? The subject is a middle-aged woman — a common woman — standing in a pool of water, in a white chemise drawn up to her thighs. It has little color, except browns and golds and the white chemise. But the flesh, one sees immediately, will in a short time have lost its firmness; already it seems to tremble, slightly, away from the bones; the woman will soon be no more woman, but merely old; this common flower will be touched by the inexorable frost; the soft golden light that seems to emanate from her body is a sunset. But how beautiful, tender, loved and lovable — how *miraculous* she is. How compact of sweetness her haunting little smile. Only a painter with a fantastic craft and technique could so have painted flesh. But not alone technique — only technique and vision — could have created the "Woman Bathing." It is a profoundly felt and realized experience.

My husband went away from it saddened and elated. Saddened with self-dissatisfaction; elated because what he feels ought to be achieved in painting was achieved. Elated to belong to, and be in the service of, so noble a craft.

All profoundly realized experience communicates — and to ordinary men. Walt Whitman said all men are poets because all respond to poetry. That is true if the people are not deprived of their natural and naïve relation to art by the abstruse and esoteric patter of professional writers about it, who patronizingly encourage the people to believe that they are incapable of understanding great expressions. When a friend, a great violinist, toured Russia, playing in villages where no artist had ever played before, he found that the people applauded for encores of Bach. No highbrows had ever told them that they could not enjoy what they did not "understand." They merely heard beautiful music. When the Soviet government opened the theaters to the workers, they did not crowd into those designed for the education of the proletariat but into the Grand Opera, the theater of kings, and above all they loved ballet — one of the most refined, and even artificial, sublimations of expression. Homer sang for common men a most uncommon song. Shakespeare wrote for the rabble and the princes. His wit was as broad as a cabby's behind and as fine as King John's delicate hair. But salt is salt on anybody's meat, if it has not lost its savor. The Bible is transcendent language and thus art, but it is still the world's best seller.

And the statesmen whom the people adore are never the ones who talk down to them, putting a twelve-foot ceiling over their words. The Declaration of Independence is not only a great democratic document but a great piece of literature. It will be on the common tongue long after the Potsdam declaration — which, having nothing worth while to say, found expression in an execrable style — is forgotten and abandoned. Yet the common people of Jefferson's day did not speak of "self-evident truths" or of a "decent respect to the opinions of mankind." Many of those to whom Jefferson's words were addressed were illiterate frontiersmen. But they understood the meaning and were proud that their hopes and strivings should find elegant and discriminating expression.

The "common man" never invented the patronizing attitude toward himself. Lincoln, the greatest people's President, was also the finest English stylist who ever occupied the White

House. The simplicity of his speeches is not the simplicity of a simpleton, but of a man with such exquisite discrimination in words that he could restore the gold tarnished from speech by vulgar use. Churchill mobilized a nation by his speeches; but they were not couched in the language of the streets, but in the highest parliamentary tradition. And Franklin Roosevelt, chosen four times by the people as their President, spoke to them in the tongue of Groton and Harvard; nor did the people hold it against him that their great friend was also a great gentleman.

So let the ceilings of democracy be high; let democratic man be aware of his own insignificance, that he may better measure his great possibilities; let him build more stately mansions for his soul. And let him know, from the examples of his times, that there is no tyranny more dreadful than that of mediocrity over distinction, of mass leaders over and through mass men, the tyranny that would reduce the people to an anthill, with a twelve-foot ceiling — and no windows on the "splendid, silent sun," the secret of whose radiation men have mastered, but whose creative beneficence is still beyond them.

Twenty-five Inches of Snow

IT STARTED during the night, and in the morning the city was white. All day long it snowed, without storm, the flakes falling silently, tenderly, but persistently. In the little garden of our old-fashioned city house, a round metal table had been left outside from the summer, and the snow, falling without wind, piled up on its surface, perfectly round, like a great fluffy white cake. It stands outside the dining room window, and as we passed through we could see how the cake was rising. When, finally, the newspapers and radio said twenty-five inches had fallen, and it was the greatest snowfall in the recorded history of New York City, we could see that the cake was just that thickness.

The snow not only blanketed the streets and the trees, burdening the buildings, piling on ledges to half-cover windows, turning wires into strings of popcorn and parked cars into streets of igloos; it blanketed sound too. When we went out into the streets the noisy, teeming metropolis was quiet as a snowbound Maine village. Not a vehicle moved or could move. Midtown, at the corner of 48th and Third, little boys were tunneling into a bank, excavating themselves a snow-house, with passages and rooms, as we used to do when children, in the country, upstate. Near Saks Fifth Avenue on that first day I saw a booted, mufflered father pulling two little girls on a sled. Such childish glees made the only clear sounds in the still air.

The first ways of passage were narrow paths on the sidewalks cut between the banks of snow. Two persons could not pass each other on these paths. One would have to step off into the deep snow. Now could be observed a phenomenon strange in New York. Nobody jostled, or glared, or pushed or shoved — no one I saw. But one could see the pantomime of people bowing to each other, smiling with the politeness of Manchu gentlemen. Each would step out of the path to face the other again, knee-deep in drift, and each would wave the other to return to the path.

In a few hours New York confronted what might become a catastrophe. In great cities where most people live in pantryless apartments, nobody keeps stores of food. If the city were not quickly cleared so that oil and coal could be delivered and food distributed from central markets to stores, people could quickly suffer cold and hunger. But there was no panic. I heard of no case of housewives plowing through the snow to buy out markets.

The mayor flew in from far away; energy radiated from City Hall; the call went out for volunteer snow shovelers, and more responded than could be employed. It was announced that it might cost three — five — seven million dollars to dig out the city, and there was not even a debate about it. Great machines, supplementing the hand shovelers, rumbled into action, pushing, lifting, moving the snow. House porters, doormen, children and householders scattered salt on the streets.

The first busses began to run, on a few streets, hugely overcrowded; but instead of glaring at new passengers, people already riding squeezed themselves cheerfully together, or reached a hand to help newcomers on. The subways were less packed than usual, for many could not get to a station. But other passengers showed, by their helplessness, their confusion and their worried studies of arrows, that they had gone underground for the first time in their lives. A lady in a mink coat so dark and rich that it rated a limousine and uniformed chauffeur praised the marvels of the subway to a Negro workman sitting opposite her, and he did not scorn her naïveté but grinned most friendlily.

The first adventurous taxi drivers crawled out and were celebrated like arctic explorers.

Busses, streetcars, shopping centers took on something of the atmosphere of the country-store cracker-barrel club. Strangers talked with one another, matching stories of discomfiture or exploit. Suddenly there had been created a community, in which everybody, without exception, was sharing a common experience, hazardous, adventurous, humorous and very inconvenient — but universal.

Then, in two days, life began to return to normal. The streets were gradually opened, wholly or partially cleared; the taxis came back in force; the delivery wagons rumbled. The piled-up snowbanks shrank under rain. The crowds shoved again. Passing one another, or sitting with one another, they glared in indifference, hostility, or boredom. The snow was dirty, and so were many looks. The crisis was over.

I have often pondered the amazing way in which people react with their best natures to a catastrophe of Nature. It is something that no one can blame on anyone else. It is most obviously not the fault of the Democrats, the Republicans, the Communists, the manufacturers, the labor unions, the rich, the poor, or the Politburo. It is "it," not "they." Being "it," it is something to be overcome by mutual energy or endured with cheerful patience. "It" unites people, instead of dividing them.

The same thing happened when, some years ago, the Mississippi burst its levees in dreadful life-snatching floods. Then, in communities where race tensions and class distinctions are normal, white men swam at great risk to rescue marooned Negroes, and Negroes, white men. There has never been a lynching during a natural catastrophe, when suddenly every life becomes precious because every life is threatened.

The struggle against Nature, when Nature appears in her less beneficent aspects, appears to furnish what William James was seeking: the moral equivalent of war. What has been called "the front spirit," because it is so familiar to soldiers, asserts itself. The presence of an enemy is apparently necessary to produce that consideration of others, that self-sacrifice which elevates men and women above their "normal" spiritual capacities and unites them in something approaching a brotherhood. This is the moral *gain* of war, to deny which would mean failure to understand one psychological element in war's recurrence, as a cement of societies.

But must mankind forever wage war on men? Must the enemy always be "they"? Cannot the enemy be "it"?

The United Nations is an arena of struggle, not cooperation. Even most of the things that the great states have agreed upon have been directed against other peoples or parts of other peoples, causing new dissensions and new human woes. Yet one instance of international cooperation, without benefit of the United Nations at all, spontaneous and genuine, has occurred in the last months, and in one of the most troubled and disputed-over sections of the world: the Middle East.

The source of the cooperation was a dreadful physical disaster: a cholera epidemic in a region where modern medicine has hardly penetrated to the masses of the people, and where there was a tragic shortage of immunization serums. Both the United States and Russia rushed to the rescue, war planes from each country flying in medical supplies, and there was no indication that anyone from either country cared a hoot whether the precious elixirs to halt the spread of the plague came out of privately or publicly owned and administered laboratories. Nor was there any disagreement about *how* to fight cholera, for though there are many ways in which societies can be constructed and many disagreements about them, medical knowledge is universally shared by physicians; each grasps eagerly and gratefully the discoveries of the other, and all agree — without veto — on such matters as quarantine, immunization, sanitation and removal of bodies.

Large parts of the world are still subject to plagues long removed from more advanced societies. Over large areas people still perish miserably from cholera, yellow fever, typhus, malaria, dreadful parasitic diseases, even smallpox and bubonic plague, though the medical arts know how to prevent, mitigate, cure or even eradicate these riders of the "pale horse" whose name is Death.

I wondered, as I watched in my home city the energy and cooperation that were called forth by twenty-five inches of snow, why the members of the United Nations do not start to cooperate on a grandiose scale, in an area where there is already unanimous agreement. Nobody — not Vishinsky, Austin, or Bevin — could even start a debate on the question: Should Cholera Be Supported?

Might not the United States, Great Britain, the Soviet Union, and the smaller states band together, therefore, against the inimical "its" — in a mutual war against the bacteria that devastate and debilitate peoples more, sometimes, than war itself?

The specter of bacteriological warfare now haunts mankind as a possible menace far worse, even, than the atom bomb. But is it conceivable that nations who had fought side by side in a war *against* bacteria, who had mobilized all their healing and preventing skills *against* the *bacterial enemy*, who had celebrated their mutually won victories in United Nations halls, the world press, and the world radios, *could* then unleash a bacteriological war against each other? Would it be psychologically possible? Could any peoples be made reconciled to it, after they had participated in a heroic effort to war against the wars bacteria wage without the help of man? I think it would be impossible, unthinkable.

Can we not wage war against the enemies of all mankind, who are not themselves human? Or will a revolting Nature prove beneficent even in her furies, and restrain men's hands from fighting each other, halting their works and frustrating their antihuman adventures by drowning them in floods, burying them in earthquakes, and silencing and restraining them behind soft, deep, impenetrable barricades of snow?